EVIDENCE-BASED TREATMENT PLANNING FOR POSTTRAUMATIC STRESS DISORDER

DVD COMPANION WORKBOOK

ARTHUR E. JONGSMA, JR.
AND
TIMOTHY J. BRUCE

John Wiley & Sons, Inc.

This book is printed on acid-free paper. ♾

Published by John Wiley & Sons, Inc., Hoboken, New Jersey.
Published simultaneously in Canada.

For general information on our other products and services please contact our Customer Care Department within the United States at (800) 762-2974, outside the United States at (317) 572-3993, or via fax at (317) 572-4002.

Wiley also publishes its books in a variety of electronic formats. Some content that appears in print may not be available in electronic books. For more information about Wiley products, visit our Web site at www.wiley.com.

ISBN 978-0-470-56852-1

Printed in the United States of America

10 9 8 7 6 5 4 3 2 1

Contents

Introduction

This *Workbook* is a companion to the Evidence-Based Treatment Planning for Posttraumatic Stress Disorder (PTSD) DVD, which is focused on informing mental health therapists, addiction counselors, and students in these fields about evidence-based psychological treatment planning.

Organization

In this *Companion Workbook* you will find in each chapter:

- ➢ Summary highlights of content shown in the DVD
- ➢ Chapter review discussion questions
- ➢ Chapter review test questions
- ➢ Chapter references

In appropriate chapters, the references are divided into those for *empirical support*, those for *clinical resources*, and those for *bibliotherapy resources*. Empirical support references are selected studies or reviews of the empirical work supporting the efficacy of the empirically supported treatments (ESTs) discussed in the chapter. The clinical resources are books, manuals, or other resources for clinicians that describe the application, or "how-to," of the treatments discussed. The bibliotherapy resources are selected publications and Web sites relevant to the DVD content that may be helpful to clinicians, clients, or laypersons.

Examples of client homework are included at www.wiley.com/go/ptsdwb. They are designed to enhance understanding of therapeutic interventions, in addition to being potentially useful clinically.

Appendix A contains an example of an evidence-based treatment plan for PTSD. In Appendix B, correct and incorrect answers to all chapter review test questions are explained.

Chapter Points

This DVD is electronically marked with chapter points that delineate the beginning of discussion sections throughout the program. You may skip to any one of these chapter points on the DVD by clicking on the forward arrow. The chapter points for this program are as follows:

- ➢ Defining PTSD
- ➢ Six Steps in Building a Psychotherapy Treatment Plan
- ➢ Brief History of the EST Movement
- ➢ ESTs for Posttraumatic Stress Disorder
- ➢ Integrating ESTs for PTSD into a Treatment Plan
- ➢ Common Considerations in Relapse Prevention
- ➢ An Evidence-Based Treatment Plan for Posttraumatic Stress Disorder

Series Rationale

Evidence-based practice (EBP) is steadily becoming the standard of mental health care, as it has of medical health care. Borrowing from the Institute of Medicine's definition (Institute of Medicine, 2001), the American Psychological Association (APA) has defined EBP as "the integration of the best available research with clinical expertise in the context of patient characteristics, culture, and preferences" (American Psychological Association Presidential Task Force on Evidence-Based Practice [APA], 2006).

Professional organizations such as the American Psychological Association, the National Association of Social Workers, and the American Psychiatric Association, as well as consumer organizations such the National Alliance for the Mentally Ill (NAMI), are endorsing EBP. At the federal level, a major joint initiative of the National Institute of Mental Health and the Department of Health and Human Services Substance Abuse and Mental Health Services Administration (SAMHSA) focuses on promoting, implementing, and evaluating evidence-based mental health programs and practices within state mental health systems (APA, 2006). In some practice settings, EBP is even becoming mandated. It is clear that the call for evidence-based practice is being increasingly sounded.

Unfortunately, many mental health care providers cannot or do not stay abreast of results from clinical research and how these results can inform their practices. Although it has rightfully been argued that the relevance of some research to the clinician's needs is weak, there are products of clinical research whose efficacy has been well-established and whose effectiveness in the community setting has received support. Clinicians and clinicians-in-training interested in empirically informing their treatments could benefit from educational programs that make this goal more easily attainable.

This series of DVDs and companion workbooks is designed to introduce clinicians and students to the process of empirically informing their psychotherapy treatment plans. The series begins with an introduction to the efforts to identify research-supported treatments and how the products of these efforts can be used to inform treatment planning. The other programs in the series focus on empirically informed treatment planning for each of several commonly seen clinical problems. In each problem-focused DVD, issues involved in defining or diagnosing the presenting problem are reviewed. Research-supported treatments for the problem are described, as well as the process used to identify them. Viewers are then systematically guided through the process of creating a treatment plan, and shown how the plan can be informed by goals, objectives, and interventions consistent with those of the identified research-supported treatments. Example vignettes of selected interventions are also provided.

This series is intended to be educational and informative in nature and not meant to be a substitute for clinical training in the specific interventions discussed and demonstrated. References to empirical support of the treatments described, clinical resource material, and training opportunities are provided.

Presenters

Dr. Art Jongsma is the Series Editor and co-author of the Practice*Planners*® Series published by John Wiley & Sons. He has authored or co-authored more than 40 books in this series. Among the books included in this series are the highly regarded *The Complete Adult Psychotherapy Treatment Planner, The Adolescent Psychotherapy Treatment Planner, The Child Psychotherapy Treatment Planner*, and *The Addiction Treatment Planner*. All of these books, along with *The Severe and Persistent Mental Illness Treatment Planner, The Family Therapy Treatment Planner, The Couples Psychotherapy Treatment Planner, The Older Adult Psychotherapy Treatment Planner,* and *The Veterans and Active Duty Military Psychotherapy Treatment Planner*, are informed with objectives and interventions that are supported by research evidence.

Dr. Jongsma also created the clinical record management software tool Thera*Scribe*®, which uses point-and-click technology to easily develop, store, and print treatment plans, progress notes, and homework assignments. He has conducted treatment planning and software training workshops for mental health professionals around the world.

Dr. Jongsma's clinical career began as a psychologist in a large private psychiatric hospital. After working in the hospital for about 10 years, he then transitioned to

Exhibit I.1 Dr. Tim Bruce and Dr. Art Jongsma

outpatient work in his own private practice clinic, Psychological Consultants, in Grand Rapids, Michigan for 25 years. He has been writing best-selling books and software for mental health professionals since 1995.

Dr. Timothy Bruce is a Professor and Associate Chair of the Department of Psychiatry and Behavioral Medicine at the University of Illinois, College of Medicine in Peoria, Illinois, where he also directs medical student education. He is a licensed clinical psychologist who completed his graduate training at SUNY-Albany, under the mentorship of Dr. David Barlow, and his residency training at Wilford Hall Medical Center, under the direction of Dr. Robert Klepac. In addition to maintaining an active clinical practice at the university, Dr. Bruce has authored numerous publications, including books, professional journal articles, book chapters, and professional educational materials, many on the topic of evidence-based practice. Most recently, he has served as the developmental editor empirically informing Dr. Jongsma's best-selling Practice*Planners*® Series.

Dr. Bruce is also Executive Director of the Center for Evidence-Based Mental Health Practices, a state- and federally funded initiative to disseminate evidence-based psychological and pharmacological practices across Illinois. Highly recognized as an educator, Dr. Bruce has received nearly two dozen awards for his teaching of students and professionals during his career.

References

American Psychological Association Presidential Task Force on Evidence-Based Practice (2006). Evidence-based practice in psychology. *American Psychologist, 61*, 271–285.

Berghuis, D., Jongsma, A., & Bruce, T. (2006). *The severe and persistent mental illness treatment planner* (2nd ed.). Hoboken, NJ: Wiley.

Dattilio, F., Jongsma, A., & Davis, S. (2009). *The family therapy treatment planner* (2nd ed.). Hoboken, NJ: Wiley.

Institute of Medicine. (2001). *Crossing the quality chasm: A new health system for the 21st century*. Washington, DC: National Academy Press.

Jongsma, A., Peterson, M., & Bruce, T. (2006). *The complete adult psychotherapy treatment planner* (4th ed.). Hoboken, NJ: Wiley.

Jongsma, A., Peterson, M., McInnis, W., & Bruce, T. (2006a). *The adolescent psychotherapy treatment planner* (4th ed.). Hoboken, NJ: Wiley.

Jongsma, A., Peterson, M., McInnis, W., & Bruce, T. (2006b). *The child psychotherapy treatment planner* (4th ed.). Hoboken, NJ: Wiley.

Moore, B., & Jongsma, A. (2009). *The veterans and active duty military psychotherapy treatment planner.* Hoboken, NJ: Wiley.

Perkinson, R., Jongsma, A., & Bruce, T. (2009). *The addiction treatment planner* (4th ed.). Hoboken, NJ: Wiley.

CHAPTER 1

What Is Posttraumatic Stress Disorder?

Defining Posttraumatic Stress Disorder

In this program, we are going to discuss evidence-based treatment planning for PTSD. Let's begin by looking at the criteria for the disorder according to the Diagnostic and Statistical Manual of Mental Disorders (DSM).

Exposure to Trauma

For PTSD, the person has to have been exposed to a traumatic event in which both of the following have been present:

1. The person has experienced, witnessed, or been confronted with an event or events that involve actual or threatened death or serious injury, or a threat to the physical integrity of oneself or others.
2. The person's response involved intense fear, helplessness, or horror. Note: in children, it may be expressed instead by disorganized or agitated behavior.

Intrusive Recollections, Avoidance/Numbing, and Hyperarousal

Exposure to the stressor is followed by a response involving symptoms from *each* of three symptom categories: intrusive recollections (Figure 1.1), avoidance/numbing (Figure 1.2), and hyperarousal (Figure 1.3).

Figure 1.1

Forms of Intrusive Recollection

Intrusive recollection means that the traumatic event is persistently reexperienced in *at least one* of the following ways:

1. Recurrent and intrusive distressing recollections of the event, including images, thoughts, or perceptions. Note: in young children, repetitive play may occur in which themes or aspects of the trauma are expressed.
2. Recurrent distressing dreams of the event. Note: in children, there may be frightening dreams without recognizable content.
3. Acting or feeling as if the traumatic event were recurring (includes a sense of reliving the experience, illusions, hallucinations, and dissociative flashback episodes, including those that occur upon awakening or when intoxicated). Note: in children, trauma-specific reenactment may occur.
4. Intense psychological distress at exposure to internal or external cues that symbolize or resemble an aspect of the traumatic event.
5. Physiologic reactivity upon exposure to internal or external cues that symbolize or resemble an aspect of the traumatic event.

Figure 1.2

Forms of Avoidance/Numbing

The second set of symptoms required for the diagnosis of PTSD reflect persistent avoidance of stimuli associated with the trauma and numbing of general responsiveness (not present before the trauma), as indicated by *at least three* of the following:

1. Efforts to avoid thoughts, feelings, or conversations associated with the trauma
2. Efforts to avoid activities, places, or people that arouse recollections of the trauma
3. Inability to recall an important aspect of the trauma
4. Markedly diminished interest or participation in significant activities
5. Feeling of detachment or estrangement from others
6. Restricted range of affect (e.g., unable to have loving feelings)
7. Sense of foreshortened future (e.g., does not expect to have a career, marriage, children, or a normal life span)

Figure 1.3

Forms of Hyperarousal

The third set of symptoms characteristic of PTSD involve persistent symptoms of increased arousal (not present before the trauma), indicated by *at least two* of the following:

1. Difficulty falling or staying asleep
2. Irritability or outbursts of anger
3. Difficulty concentrating
4. Hypervigilance
5. Exaggerated startle response

Duration of Symptoms

To meet criteria for PTSD, the duration of this response (involving symptoms from each of the three symptom categories just discussed) must be more than one month.

Distress or Disability

As with any mental-emotional disorder, the symptoms of PTSD must cause clinically significant distress or impairment in social, occupational, or other important areas of functioning.

Specifiers

- Specifiers used with the diagnosis of PTSD include whether it is chronic or acute, and whether it is with or without a delay in onset.
- The condition is considered acute if the duration of symptoms has been *less than three months* and chronic if it has been *three months or more.*
- Delayed onset refers to symptoms whose onset occurred *after six months* from exposure to the traumatic stressor.

Diagnostic Criteria for PTSD

A summary of the diagnostic criteria for PTSD can be found in Figure 1.4.

Figure 1.4

Diagnostic Criteria Summary for Posttraumatic Stress Disorder

Criterion A: Exposure to Traumatic Stressor
Criterion B: Intrusive Recollections of Trauma
Criterion C: Avoidance of Trauma-Related Stimuli, Numbing of General Responsiveness
Criterion D: Hyperarousal
Criterion E: Duration (at least one month)
Criterion F: Clinical Distress or Disability

SPECIFIERS:

- Acute = Symptoms less than 3 months
- Chronic = Symptoms more than 3 months
- With or Without Delayed Onset (6 months after trauma)

From *The Diagnostic and Statistical Manual of Mental Disorders-IV-TR* (APA, 2000).

Chapter Review

1. What are the diagnostic criteria for posttraumatic stress disorder?

Chapter Review Test Questions

1. Which of the following does not represent one of the three categories of diagnostic *symptoms* of PTSD?

   A. Experiencing an event that involved threatened death
   B. Feeling of detachment or estrangement from others
   C. Irritability or outbursts of anger
   D. Recurrent distressing dreams of the event

2. The DSM diagnosis, "Posttraumatic Stress Disorder, Acute (309.81)," means that the symptoms of PTSD have been present for how long?

   A. Less than one month
   B. More than one month, but less than six months
   C. More than one month, but less than three months
   D. More than six months

Chapter Reference

American Psychiatric Association. (2000). *Diagnostic and statistical manual of mental disorders* (4th ed., text revised). Washington, DC: American Psychiatric Association.

CHAPTER 2

What Are the Six Steps in Building a Psychotherapy Treatment Plan?

Step 1: Identify primary and secondary problems

- ➢ Use evidence-based psychosocial assessment procedures to determine the most significant problem or problems related to current distress, disability, or both.

Step 2: Describe the problem's manifestations (symptom pattern)

- ➢ Note how the problem(s) are evidenced your particular client. These features may correspond to the diagnostic criteria for the problem.

Step 3: Make a diagnosis based on DSM/ICD criteria

- ➢ Based on an evaluation of the client's complete clinical presentation, determine the appropriate diagnosis using the process and criteria described in the DSM or the ICD.

Step 4: Specify long-term goals

- ➢ These goal statements need not be crafted in measurable terms, but are broader and indicate a desired general positive outcome of treatment.

Step 5: Create short-term objectives

- ➢ Objectives for the client to achieve should be stated in measurable or observable terms so accountability is enhanced.

Step 6: Select therapeutic interventions

- ➢ Interventions are the actions of the clinician within the therapeutic alliance designed to help the client accomplish the treatment objectives. There should be at least one intervention planned for each client objective.

Key Point

One important aspect of effective treatment planning is that each plan should be tailored to the individual client's particular problems and needs. Treatment plans should not be boilerplate, even if clients have similar problems. Consistent with the definition of an evidence-based practice, the individual's strengths and weaknesses, unique stressors, cultural and social network, family circumstances, and symptom patterns must be considered in developing a treatment strategy. Clinicians should rely on their own good clinical judgment and plan a treatment that is appropriate for the distinctive individual with whom they are working.

Chapter Review

1. What are the six steps involved in developing a psychotherapy treatment plan?

Chapter Review Test Questions

1. The diagnosis of PTSD requires the evidence of hyperarousal, but clients may experience this in different ways. For example, some will have a sleep disturbance; others may be irritable or startle easily. In which step of treatment planning would you record these features of your particular client?
   A. Creating short-term objectives
   B. Describing the problem's manifestations
   C. Identifying the primary problem
   D. Selecting treatment interventions

2. The statement "Identify, challenge, and change biased self-talk supportive of depression" is an example of which of the following steps in a treatment plan?
   A. A primary problem
   B. A short-term objective
   C. A symptom manifestation
   D. A treatment intervention

Chapter References

American Psychological Association Presidential Task Force on Evidence-Based Practice. (2006). Evidence-based practice in psychology. *American Psychologist, 61*, 271–285.

Jongsma, A. (2005). Psychotherapy treatment plan writing. In G. P. Koocher, J. C. Norcross, & S. S. Hill (Eds.), *Psychologists' desk reference* (2nd ed., pp. 232–236). New York, NY: Oxford University Press.

Jongsma, A. Peterson, M., & Bruce, T. (2006). *The complete adult psychotherapy treatment planner* (4th ed.). Hoboken, NJ: Wiley.

Jongsma, A., Peterson, M., McInnis, W., & Bruce, T. (2006). *The adolescent psychotherapy treatment planner* (4th ed.). Hoboken, NJ: Wiley.

CHAPTER 3

What Is the Brief History of the Empirically Supported Treatments Movement?

In the United States, the effort to identify empirically supported treatments (EST) began with an initiative of the American Psychological Association's Division 12—The Society of Clinical Psychology.

In 1993, APA's Division 12 President David Barlow initiated a task group, chaired by Diane Chambless. The group was charged to review the psychotherapy outcome literature to identify psychological treatments whose efficacy had been demonstrated through clinical research. This group was originally called the Task Force on the Promotion and Dissemination of Psychological Procedures, and was later reorganized under the Task Force on Psychological Interventions.

Process Used to Identify Empirically Supported Treatments

Reviewers established two primary sets of criteria for judging the evidence base supporting any particular therapy. One was labeled *well-established*, the other *probably efficacious* (Figure 3.1).

Figure 3.1

Specific Criteria for Well-Established and Probably Efficacious Treatments

Criteria for a Well-Established Treatment

For a psychological treatment to be considered *well-established*, the evidence base supporting it had to be characterized by the following:

I. At least two, good between group design experiments demonstrating efficacy in one or more of the following ways
   A. Superior (statistically significantly so) to pill or psychological placebo or to another treatment
   B. Equivalent to an already established treatment in experiments with adequate sample sizes

(*continued*)

OR

II. A large series of single case design experiments (n > 9) demonstrating efficacy. These experiments must have:

A. Used good experimental designs

B. Compared the intervention to another treatment, as in IA

Further Criteria for Both I and II

III. Experiments must be conducted with treatment manuals.

IV. Characteristics of the client samples must be clearly specified.

V. Effects must have been demonstrated by at least two different investigators or investigating teams.

Criteria for a Probably Efficacious Treatment

For a psychological treatment to be considered *probably efficacious*, the evidence base supporting it had to meet the following criteria:

I. Two experiments showing the treatment is superior (statistically significantly so) to a waiting-list control group.

OR

II. One or more experiments meeting the well-established treatment criteria IA or IB, III, and IV, but not V.

OR

III. A small series of single case design experiments (n > 3) otherwise meeting Well-Established Treatment

Adapted from "Update on Empirically Validated Therapies, II," by D. L. Chambless, M. J. Baker, D. H. Baucom, L. E. Beutler, K. S. Calhoun, P. Crits-Christoph, . . . S. R. Woody, 1998, *The Clinical Psychologist, 51*(1), 3–16.

Key Point

Division 12's criteria for a well-established treatment are similar to the standards used by the United States Food and Drug Administration (FDA) to evaluate the safety and efficacy of proposed medications. The FDA requires demonstration that a proposed medication is significantly superior to a nonspecific control treatment (a pill placebo) in at least two randomized controlled trials conducted by independent research groups. Division 12's criteria for a well-established treatment requires the equivalent of this standard as well as other features relevant to judging a psychological treatment's efficacy (e.g., a clear description of the treatment and study participants). By extension, if the FDA were to evaluate psychotherapies using the criteria they use for medication, it would allow sale of those judged to be well-established.

Products of Empirically Supported Treatment Reviews

The products of these reviews can be found in the Division 12 groups' final two reports.

- In the first report, 47 ESTs were identified (Chambless, et al., 1996).
- In the final report, the list had grown to 71 ESTs (Chambless, et al., 1998).
- In 1999, The Society of Clinical Psychology, Division 12, took full ownership of maintaining the growing list. The current list and information center can be found on its Web site, at www.psychologicaltreatments.org.

Around this same time, other groups emerged, using the same or similar criteria, to review literatures related to other populations, problems, and interventions. Examples include the following:

- Children (Lonigan & Elbert, 1998)
- Pediatric Psychology (Spirito, 1999)
- Older Adults (Gatz, 1998)
- Adult, Child, Marital, Family Therapy (Kendall & Chambless, 1998)
- Psychopharmacology and Psychological Treatments (Nathan & Gorman, 1998; 2002; 2007)

For those interested in comparing and contrasting the criteria used by various review groups, see Chambless and Ollendick (2001).

TherapyAdvisor

Descriptions of the treatments identified through many of these early reviews, as well as references to the empirical work supporting them, clinical resources, and training opportunities, can be found at www.therapyadvisor.com. This resource was developed by Personal Improvement Computer Systems (PICS) with funding from the National Institute of Mental Health and in consultation with members of the original Division 12 task groups. Information found on TherapyAdvisor is provided by the primary author/researcher(s) of the given EST.

Selected Organizational Reviewers of Evidence-Based Psychological Treatments and Practices

- The United Kingdom is on the forefront of the effort to identify evidence-based treatments and develop guidelines for practice. The latest products of their work can be found at the Web site for the National Institute for Health and Clinical Excellence (NICE): www.nice.org.uk.

- The Substance Abuse and Mental Health Service Administration, or SAMHSA, has an initiative to evaluate, identify, and provide information on various mental health practices. Their work, entitled "The National Registry of Evidence-based Programs and Practices or NREPP," can be found online at www.nrepp.samhsa.gov.
- The Agency for Health Care Policy and Research, now called the Agency for Healthcare Research and Quality (AHRQ), has established guidelines and criteria for identifying evidence-based practices and provides links to evidence-based clinical practice guidelines for various medical and mental health problems at www.ahrq.gov/clinic/epcix.htm.

Chapter Review

1. How did Division 12 of the APA identify ESTs?
2. What are the primary differences between *well-established* and *probably efficacious* criteria used to identify ESTs?
3. Where can information about ESTs and evidence-based practices be found?

Chapter Review Test Questions

1. Which statement best describes the process used to identify empirically supported treatments (ESTs)?

   A. Consumers of mental health services nominated therapies.
   B. Experts came to a consensus based on their experiences with the treatments.
   C. Researchers submitted their works.
   D. Task groups reviewed the literature using clearly defined selection criteria for ESTs.

2. Based on the differences in their criteria, in which of the following ways are well-established treatments different than those classified as probably efficacious?

   A. Only probably efficacious treatments allowed the use of a single case design experiment.
   B. Only well-established treatments allowed studies comparing the treatment to a psychological placebo.
   C. Only well-established treatments required demonstration by at least two different, independent investigators or investigating teams.
   D. Only well-established treatments allowed studies comparing the treatment to a pill placebo.

Chapter References

Chambless, D. L., Baker, M. J., Baucom, D. H., Beutler, L. E., Calhoun, K. S., Crits-Christoph, P., . . . Woody, S. R. (1998). Update on empirically validated therapies, II. *The Clinical Psychologist, 51*, 3–16.

Chambless, D. L., & Ollendick, T. H. (2001). Empirically supported psychological interventions: Controversies and evidence. *Annual Review of Psychology, 52*, 685–716.

Chambless, D. L., Sanderson, W. C., Shoham, V., Bennett Johnson, S., Pope, K. S., Crits-Christoph, P., . . . McCurry, S. (1996). An update on empirically validated therapies. *The Clinical Psychologist, 49*, 5–18.

Gatz, M., Fiske, A., Fox, L. S., Kaskie, B., Kasl-Godley, J. E., McCallum, T., & Wetherell, J. (1998). Empirically validated psychological treatments for older adults. *Journal of Mental Health and Aging, 41*, 9–46.

Kendall, P. C., & Chambless, D. L. (Eds.). (1998). Empirically supported psychological therapies [special issue]. *Journal of Consulting and Clinical Psychology, 66*(3), 151–162.

Lonigan, C. J., & Elbert, J. C. (Eds.). (1998). Empirically supported psychosocial interventions for children [special issue]. *Journal of Clinical Child Psychology, 27*, 138–226.

Nathan, P. E., & Gorman, J. M. (Eds.). (1998). *A guide to treatments that work.* New York, NY: Oxford University Press.

Nathan, P. E., & Gorman, J. M. (Eds.). (2002). *A guide to treatments that work* (2nd ed.). New York, NY: Oxford University Press.

Nathan, P. E., & Gorman, J. M. (Eds.). (2007). *A guide to treatments that work* (3rd ed.). New York, NY: Oxford University Press.

Spirito, A. (Ed.). (1999). Empirically supported treatments in pediatric psychology [special issue]. *Journal of Pediatric Psychology, 24*, 87–174.

CHAPTER 4

What Are the Identified Empirically Supported Treatments for Posttraumatic Stress Disorder?

Empirically informing a treatment plan as described in this series involves integrating those aspects of identified ESTs into each step of the treatment planning process discussed previously. Let's briefly look at efforts to develop and identify ESTs and evidence-based treatment guidelines for PTSD.

The psychotherapy outcome literature in PTSD has grown significantly over the last decade. There have been several independent reviews of this literature that have identified empirically supported treatments and/or treatment guidelines for PTSD. Although the conclusions and recommendations of these various reviewers are highly similar, there are some notable differences largely dependent on the criteria used by the reviewers.

The Society of Clinical Psychology

Using the most rigorous criteria of all reviewers, APA's Division 12 (The Society of Clinical Psychology) has identified three therapies that have met their original criteria for a *well-established* EST. These treatment approaches are:

- Prolonged exposure
- Cognitive processing therapy (a treatment that combines exposure and cognitive restructuring)
- Eye movement desensitization and reprocessing (EMDR)

All of these treatments are *trauma-focused,* meaning that they focus on helping the client process the memory of the trauma.

Division 12 has also identified one therapeutic approach as having met their criteria for a *probably efficacious* treatment. This therapy is called stress inoculation training. Stress inoculation training (SIT) is not trauma-focused, but rather present-focused and helps train skills intended to facilitate the client's current adaptive functioning.

Figure 4.1

Conclusions From the Society of Clinical Psychology Review

WELL-ESTABLISHED ESTs FOR PTSD

- Prolonged exposure
- Cognitive processing therapy (a treatment that combines exposure and cognitive restructuring)
- Eye movement desensitization and reprocessing (EMDR)

Note: All of these treatments are *trauma-focused*, meaning that they focus on helping the client process the memory of the trauma.

PROBABLY EFFICACIOUS EST

- Stress inoculation training

Note: Stress inoculation training is not trauma-focused, but rather helps train skills intended to facilitate the client's current adaptive functioning.

From The Society of Clinical Psychology (APA Division 12). Available online at: www.psychologicaltreatments.org

Figure 4.1 provides a synopsis of conclusions drawn from the Society of Clinical Psychology reviews.

Ponniah and Hollon Review

Another recent and independent review was conducted by Ponniah and Hollon (2009) using, in part, criteria equivalent to those used by Division 12 for a well-established EST. These reviewers concluded that trauma-focused cognitive behavioral therapies that use exposure with or without cognitive restructuring meet the criteria for a well-established EST. Although noting that it has a lesser body of supporting evidence, these reviewers also cited EMDR as meeting these same criteria. This conclusion replicates that of Division 12's previously discussed.

Stress inoculation training was again judged as showing efficacy, but not at a level warranting its status as a well-established EST. These reviewers categorized it as *possibly efficacious*, using criteria less rigorous than the criteria for *probably efficacious* used by Division 12.

Ponniah and Holon (2009) also noted that one or a few nonindependent trials have shown support for an exposure-oriented form of hypnotherapy, interpersonal therapy, and brief psychodynamic therapy—all in comparison to wait-list control groups. They noted that the evidence supporting these last three therapies is preliminary and that they would need further study to support stronger conclusions regarding their efficacy.

Figure 4.2

Conclusions From the Ponniah and Hollon Review

WELL-ESTABLISHED ESTs FOR PTSD

- Trauma-focused cognitive behavioral therapies that use exposure with or without cognitive restructuring

Note: Category is inclusive of well-established ESTs identified by APA's Division 12.

POSSIBLY EFFICACIOUS ESTs

- Stress inoculation training
- Exposure-oriented hypnotherapy
- Interpersonal therapy
- Brief psychodynamic therapy

Note: The *possibly efficacious* category is more inclusive and less rigorous than the *probably efficacious* category used by APA's Division 12. *Possibly efficacious* means, "Pending replication, if there was just one study providing evidence of efficacy or if all the research had been carried out in one setting" (p.1088).

LITTLE EVIDENCE TO SUPPORT THE USE OF THESE TREATMENTS

- Relaxation training (alone)
- Group CBT
- Family therapy
- Supportive counseling

From "Empirically Supported Psychological Treatments for Adult Acute Stress Disorder and Posttraumatic Stress Disorder: A Review," by K. Ponniah and S. D. Hollon, 2009, *Depression and Anxiety, 26,* 1086–1109.

Lastly, these reviewers noted that they found little evidence to support the use of relaxation training alone, CBT delivered in a group format, family therapy, or supportive counseling.

Figure 4.2 provides a synopsis of conclusions drawn from the Ponniah and Hollon review.

The National Institute for Health and Clinical Excellence

As mentioned previously, The National Institute for Health and Clinical Excellence (NICE) in the United Kingdom conducts extensive literature reviews and publishes practical evidence-based guidelines for the treatment of various medical and mental health problems. Their guidelines for the treatment of PTSD reflect a first-line emphasis on the well-established, trauma-focused ESTs such as those identified by APA's Division 12 and Ponniah and Hollon (2009). For example, among several specific guidelines for the treatment of PTSD they provide, NICE states:

- "All PTSD sufferers should be offered a course of trauma-focused psychological treatment (trauma-focused cognitive–behavioural therapy or eye movement desensitisation and reprocessing)."
- "These treatments should normally be provided on an individual out-patient basis."
- "Some PTSD sufferers may initially find it difficult and overwhelming to disclose details of their traumatic events. In these cases, healthcare professionals should consider devoting several sessions to establishing a trusting therapeutic relationship and emotional stabilisation before addressing the traumatic event."
- "When PTSD sufferers request other forms of psychological treatment (for example, supportive therapy/non-directive therapy, hypnotherapy, psychodynamic therapy or systemic psychotherapy), they should be informed that there is as yet no convincing evidence for a clinically important effect of these treatments on PTSD."
- "Non-trauma-focused interventions such as relaxation or non-directive therapy, which do not address traumatic memories, should *not* routinely be offered to people who present with chronic PTSD."

Figure 4.3 provides a synopsis of recommendations from the NICE guidelines.

Figure 4.3

Recommendations From The National Institute for Health and Clinical Excellence (NICE)

RECOMMENDED FIRST-LINE OPTIONS

- Trauma-focused psychological treatment (trauma-focused cognitive–behavioural therapy or eye movement desensitization and reprocessing).

Available online at: www.nice.org.uk

International Society for Traumatic Stress Studies (ISTSS)

Other reviewers have used criteria less rigorous than Division 12's for a well-established EST. These criteria value high quality RCTs, but do not require the independent replication of results that Division 12's criteria for *well-established* do. Accordingly, reviewers using these criteria have drawn more inclusive conclusions regarding empirically supported treatment options for PTSD. One example is found in the guidelines for the treatment of PTSD copyrighted by the International Society for Traumatic Stress Studies (ISTSS).

- ➢ These guidelines conclude that CBT comprising exposure therapy, cognitive therapy, stress inoculation training, or therapies that combine exposure with formal cognitive therapy or stress inoculation training should all be considered first-line options for the treatment of PTSD in addition to EMDR, which was also indicated as an appropriate first-line option.
- ➢ The guidelines further state that relaxation training, biofeedback, and other adaptive skills training (such as assertiveness skill training) cannot be recommended as stand-alone therapies for PTSD, but may have potential benefit as adjuncts to those treatments judged first-line.
- ➢ Consistent with the NICE guidelines and Ponniah and Hollon's findings regarding the lack of evidence for group-format therapy, the guidelines recommend that the treatments discussed should be delivered through one-on-one therapy.
- ➢ As can be seen, the ISTSS guidelines are more inclusive of present-focused (non-trauma-focused) treatments (e.g., stress inoculation training) in first-line options than other guideline developers such as NICE.

Figure 4.4 provides a synopsis of recommendations from the ISTSS guidelines.

Figure 4.4

Recommendations From the International Society for Traumatic Stress Studies

Recommended First-Line Options:

- Exposure therapy
- Cognitive therapy
- Stress inoculation training
- Therapies that combine exposure with cognitive therapy or stress inoculation training
- Eye movement desensitization and reprocessing

Adjunctive Treatment Components (not stand-alone treatments):

- Relaxation training
- Biofeedback
- Adaptive skills training (such as assertiveness skill training)

From "Effective Treatments for Posttraumatic Stress Disorder: Practice Guidelines from the International Society for Traumatic Stress Studies" (2nd ed.), by E. B. Foa, T. M. Keane, M. J. Friedman, and J. A. Cohen, 2009, New York, NY: Guilford Press.

Najavits Review

In the latest edition of Nathan and Gorman's *A Guide to Treatments That Work*, Najavits (2007) came to conclusions similar to the ISTSS using similar criteria (Figure 4.5).

- ➢ Najavits advanced that trauma-focused therapies such as exposure, EMDR, and some applications of cognitive therapy as well as more present-focused therapies such as SIT should all be considered first-line options and as such allow therapists some latitude in first-line choice.

- Najavits also noted, however, that combining any of these therapies, although intuitively appealing, has shown no greater efficacy in the clinical research literature than delivering any one of them alone.

Figure 4.5 provides a synopsis of conclusions drawn from the Najavits review.

Figure 4.5

Conclusions From the Najavits Review

Recommended First-Line Options

- Trauma-focused therapies (e.g., exposure, EMDR, cognitive therapy)
- Present-focused therapies (e.g., stress inoculation training)
- Notes that combination therapies have shown no greater efficacy in the clinical research literature than delivering any one of them alone.

From "Psychosocial Treatments for Posttraumatic Stress Disorder," by L. M. Najavits, 2007. In P. E. Nathan and J. M. Gorman (Eds.), *A Guide to Treatments that Work* (3rd ed., pp. 513–530). New York, NY: Oxford University Press.

Conclusions

In demonstrating evidence-based treatment planning, we use the definition of an evidence-based practice advanced by the American Psychological Association, which states that it is "the integration of the best available research with clinical expertise, in the context of patient characteristics, culture, and preferences."

Reviewers of the treatment outcome literature for PTSD that used the most rigorous criteria conclude that trauma-focused CBT involving exposure with or without cognitive restructuring as well as EMDR are treatments whose efficacy is well-established. Present-focused treatments such as SIT were judged to have empirical support, but at a lower level of evidence. Guideline developers such as NICE that use similar criteria also recommend trauma-focused treatments as first-line considerations. They recommend that present-focused treatments be considered only if the client is unable to participate in a trauma-focused therapy.

Other reviewers whose criteria did not require independent replication include present-focused treatments such as SIT among first-line options. Guideline developers using similar criteria have made similar recommendations.

For our purposes in demonstrating evidence-based treatment planning, we provide examples drawn from both trauma-focused and present-focused ESTs. Given the best available evidence, either could be used justifiably, given the circumstances, as part of an evidence-based practice.

Chapter Review

1. Reviewers of the PTSD treatment outcome literature who used criteria for a well-established EST, requiring independent replication (e.g., The Society of Clinical Psychology, Ponniah & Hollon, 2009), identified which therapies as well-established?
2. How did the conclusion drawn by reviewers whose criteria did not require independent replication differ from those whose criteria did?

Chapter Review Test Questions

1. Which of the following is not a trauma-focused intervention for PTSD?
   A. Cognitive processing therapy (CPT)
   B. Eye movement desensitization and reprocessing (EMDR)
   C. Prolonged exposure (PE)
   D. Stress inoculation training (SIT)

2. Which form of exposure is used *prominently* in trauma-focused treatments for PTSD?
   A. Imaginal exposure
   B. Live exposure (*in vivo*)
   C. Simulated exposure (role-played)
   D. Virtual reality exposure

Selected Chapter References

Reviews of the PTSD Outcome Literature

Foa, E. B., Keane, T. M., Friedman, M. J., & Cohen, J. A. (2009). *Effective treatments for posttraumatic stress disorder: Practice guidelines from the International Society for Traumatic Stress Studies* (2nd ed.). New York, NY: Guilford Press.

Najavits, L. M. (2007). Psychosocial treatments for posttraumatic stress disorder. In P. E. Nathan & J. M. Gorman (Eds.), *A guide to treatments that work* (pp. 513–530). New York, NY: Oxford University Press.

Ponniah, K., & Hollon, S. D. (2009) Empirically supported psychological treatments for adult acute stress disorder and posttraumatic stress disorder: A review. *Depression and Anxiety, 26*, 1086–1109.

Empirical Support for Trauma-Focused Cognitive Behavioral Therapy Involving Exposure and/or Cognitive Restructuring

Bryant, R. A., Moulds, M. L., Guthrie, R. M., Dang, S. T., & Nixon, R. D. (2003). Imaginal exposure alone and imaginal exposure with cognitive restructuring in treatment of posttraumatic stress disorder. *Journal of Consulting and Clinical Psychology, 71*, 706–712.

Chard, K. M. (2005). An evaluation of cognitive processing therapy for the treatment of posttraumatic stress disorder related to childhood sexual abuse. *Journal of Consulting and Clinical Psychology, 73*, 965–971.

Cottraux, J., Note, I., Yao, S. N., de Mey-Guillard, C., Bonasse, F., Djamoussian, D., . . . Chen, Y. (2008). Randomized controlled comparison of cognitive behavior therapy with Rogerian supportive therapy in chronic post-traumatic stress disorder: A 2-year follow-up. *Psychotherapy and Psychosomatics, 77*, 101–110.

Echeburua, E., de Corral, P., Zubizarreta, I., & Sarasua, B. (1997). Psychological treatment of chronic posttraumatic stress disorder in victims of sexual aggression. *Behavior Modification, 21*, 433–456.

Foa, E. B., Dancu, C. V., Hembree, E. A., Jaycox, L. H., Meadows, E. A., & Street, G. P. (1999). A comparison of exposure therapy, stress inoculation training, and their combination for reducing posttraumatic stress disorder in female assault victims. *Journal of Consulting and Clinical Psychology, 67*, 194–200.

Foa, E. B., Hembree, E. A., Cahill, S. P., Rauch, S. A. M., Riggs, D. S., Feeny, N. C., & Yadin, E. (2005). Randomized trial of prolonged exposure for posttraumatic stress disorder with and without cognitive restructuring: Outcome at academic and community clinics. *Journal of Consulting and Clinical Psychology, 73*, 953–964.

Foa, E. B., Rothbaum, B. O., Riggs, D., & Murdock, T. (1991). Treatment of posttraumatic stress disorder in rape victims: A comparison between cognitive-behavioral procedures and counseling. *Journal of Consulting and Clinical Psychology, 59*, 715–723.

Keane, T. M., Fairbank, J. A., Caddell, J. M., & Zimering, R. T. (1989). Implosive (flooding) therapy reduces symptoms of PTSD in Vietnam combat veterans. *Behavior Therapy, 20*, 245–260.

Litz, B. T., Engel, C. C., Bryant, R. A., & Papa, A. (2007). A randomized, controlled proof-of-concept trial of an internet-based, therapist-assisted self-management treatment for posttraumatic stress disorder. *American Journal of Psychiatry, 164*, 1676–1683.

Marks, I., Lovell, K., Noshirvani, H., Livanou, M., & Thrasher, S. (1998). Treatment of posttraumatic stress disorder by exposure and/or cognitive restructuring. *Archives of General Psychiatry, 55*, 317–325.

Monson, C. M., Schnurr, P. P., Resick, P. A., Friedman, M. J., Young-Xu, Y., & Stevens, S. P. (2006). Cognitive processing therapy for veterans with military-related posttraumatic stress disorder. *Journal of Consulting and Clinical Psychology, 74*, 898–907.

Neuner, F., Schauer, M., Klaschik, C., Karunakara, U., & Elbert, T. (2004). A comparison of narrative exposure therapy, supportive counseling, and psychoeducation for treating posttraumatic stress disorder in an African refugee settlement. *Journal of Consulting and Clinical Psychology, 72*, 579–587.

Paunovic, N. (2002). Prolonged exposure counterconditioning (PEC) as a treatment of chronic posttraumatic stress disorder and major depression in an adult survivor of repeated child sexual and physical abuse. *Clinical Case Studies, 1*, 148–169.

Resick, P. A., Galovski, T. E., Uhlmansiek, M. O., Scher, C. D., Clum, G. A., & Young-Xu, Y. (2008). A randomized clinical trial to dismantle components of cognitive processing therapy for posttraumatic stress disorder in female victims of interpersonal violence. *Journal of Consulting and Clinical Psychology, 76*, 243–258.

Resick, P. A., Nishith, P., Weaver, T. L., Astin, M. C., & Feuer, C. A. (2002). A comparison of cognitive-processing therapy with prolonged exposure and a waiting condition for the treatment of chronic posttraumatic stress disorder in female rape victims. *Journal of Consulting and Clinical Psychology, 70,* 867–879.

Schnurr, P. P., Friedman, M. J., Engel, C. C., Foa, E. B., Shea, M. T., Chow, B. K., . . . Bernardy, N. (2007). Cognitive behavioral therapy for posttraumatic stress disorder in women: a randomized controlled trial. *Journal of the American Medical Association, 297,* 820–830.

Taylor, S., Thordarson, D. S., Maxfield, L., Fedoroff, I. C., Lovell, K., & Ogrodniczuk, J. (2003). Comparative efficacy, speed, and adverse effects of three PTSD treatments: exposure therapy, EMDR, and relaxation training. *Journal of Consulting and Clinical Psychology, 71*(2), 330–338.

Tarrier, N., Pilgrim, H., Sommerfield, C., Faragher, B., Reynolds, M., Graham, E., & Barrowclough, C. (1999). A randomized trial of cognitive therapy and imaginal exposure in the treatment of chronic posttraumatic stress disorder. *Journal of Consulting and Clinical Psychology, 67,* 13–18.

Tarrier, N., & Sommerfield, C. (2004). Treatment of chronic PTSD by cognitive therapy and exposure: Five-year follow-up. *Behavior Therapy, 35,* 231–246.

Van Arntz, A., Minnen, A, & Keijsers, G. P. J. (2002). Prolonged exposure in patients with chronic PTSD: Predictors of treatment outcome and dropout. *Behaviour Research and Therapy, 40,* 439–457.

Clinical Resources

Foa, E., Chrestman, K. R., & Gilboa-Schectman, E. (2008). *Prolonged exposure therapy for adolescents with PTSD* (therapist guide). New York, NY: Oxford University Press.

Foa, E., Hembree, E., & Rothbaum, B. (2007). *Prolonged exposure therapy for PTSD: Emotional processing of traumatic experiences (therapist guide).* New York, NY: Oxford University Press.

Resick, P. A., & Calhoun, K. S. (2001). Posttraumatic stress disorder. In D. H. Barlow (Ed.), *Clinical handbook of psychological disorders: A step-by-step treatment manual* (3rd ed., pp. 60–113). New York, NY: Guilford Press.

Resick, P. A., & Schnicke, M. K. (1993). *Cognitive processing therapy for rape victims: A treatment manual.* Newbury Park, CA: Sage.

Smith, P., Perrin, S., Yule, W., & Clark, D. M. (2009). *Post traumatic stress disorder: Cognitive therapy with children and young people.* New York, NY: Routledge.

Smyth, L. (2008). *Overcoming post-traumatic stress disorder: A cognitive-behavioral exposure-based protocol for the treatment of PTSD and the other anxiety disorders.* Oakland, CA: New Harbinger.

Taylor, S. (2009). *Clinician's guide to PTSD: A cognitive-behavioral approach.* New York, NY: Guilford Press.

Cognitive Processing Therapy Web-based learning course at: http://cpt.musc.edu/index

Workshop and Training Opportunities

National Center for PTSD
Dissemination and Training Division
VA Palo Alto Health Care System
Menlo Park, CA 94025
www.ptsd.va.gov/about/divisions/dissemination-training-division.asp

Behavioral Science Division (116B-2)
VA Boston Healthcare System
150 South Huntington Avenue
Boston, MA 02130
www.ptsd.va.gov/about/divisions/behavioral-science-division.asp

Women's Health Sciences Division (116B-3)
VA Boston Healthcare System
150 South Huntington Avenue
Boston, MA 02130
www.ptsd.va.gov/about/divisions/womens-health-sciences-division.asp

National Crime Victims Research and Treatment Center
Department of Psychiatry and Behavioral Sciences
Medical University of South Carolina
67 President Street, MSC 861
2nd Floor IOP South Building
Charleston, SC 29403
http://colleges.musc.edu/ncvc/

Center for the Treatment and Study of Anxiety
University of Pennsylvania
3535 Market Street, 6th floor
Philadelphia, PA 19104
www.med.upenn.edu/ctsa/

The Association for Behavioral and Cognitive Therapies has offered training workshops in cognitive processing therapy for PTSD at its annual conference (for more information see www.abct.org).

Empirical Support for Eye Movement Desensitization and Reprocessing

Boudewyns, P. A., Stwertka, S. A., Hyer, L. A., Albrecht, J. W., & Sperr, E. V. (1993). Eye movement desensitization for PTSD of combat: A treatment outcome pilot study. *The Behavior Therapist, 16,* 29–33.

Carlson, J. G., Chemtob, C. M., Rusnak, K., Hedlund, N. L., & Muraoka, M. Y. (1998). Eye movement desensitization and reprocessing (EMDR) treatment for combat-related posttraumatic stress disorder. *Journal of Traumatic Stress, 11,* 3–24.

Devilly, G. J., & Spence, S. H. (1999). The relative efficacy and treatment distress of EMDR and a cognitive behavioral trauma treatment protocol in the amelioration of posttraumatic stress disorder. *Journal of Anxiety Disorders, 13,* 131–157.

Jensen, J. A. (1994). An investigation of eye movement desensitization and reprocessing (EMDR) as a treatment of posttraumatic stress disorder (PTSD) symptoms of Vietnam combat veterans. *Behavior Therapy, 25,* 311–325.

Lee, C., Gavriel, H., Drummond, P., Richards, J., & Greenwald, R. (2002). Treatment of post-traumatic stress disorder: A comparison of stress inoculation training with prolonged exposure and eye movement desensitization and reprocessing. *Journal of Clinical Psychology, 58,* 1071–1089.

Power, K. G., McGoldrick, T., Brown, K., Buchanan, R., Sharp, D., Swanson, V., & Karatzias, A. (2002). A controlled comparison of eye movement desensitisation and reprocessing versus exposure plus cognitive restructuring, versus waiting list in the treatment of posttraumatic stress disorder. *Journal of Clinical Psychology and Psychotherapy, 9,* 299–318.

Rothbaum, B. O. (1997). A controlled study of eye movement desensitization and reprocessing in the treatment of posttraumatic stress disordered sexual assault victims. *Bulletin of the Menninger Clinic, 61,* 317–334.

van der Kolk, B. A., Spinazzola, J., Blaustein, M. E., Hopper, J. W., Hopper, E. K., Korn, D. L., & Simpson, W. B. (2007). A randomized clinical trial of eye movement desensitization and reprocessing (EMDR), fluoxetine, and pill placebo in the treatment of posttraumatic stress disorder: Treatment effects and long-term maintenance. *Journal of Clinical Psychiatry, 68,* 37–46.

Wilson, S. A., Becker, L. A., & Tinker, R. H. (1995). Eye movement desensitization and reprocessing (EMDR) treatment for psychologically traumatized individuals. *Journal of Consulting and Clinical Psychology, 63,* 928–937.

Clinical Resources

Shapiro, F. (2001). *Eye movement desensitization and reprocessing: basic principles, protocols and procedures* (2nd ed.). New York, NY: Guilford Press.

Workshop and Training Opportunities

The EMDR Institute in Watsonville, CA offers training in EMDR (for more information, see www.emdr.com).

Empirical Evidence for Stress Inoculation Training

Foa, E. B., Dancu, C. V., Hembree, E. A., Jaycox, L. H., Meadows, E. A., & Street, G. P. (1999). A comparison of exposure therapy, stress inoculation training, and their combination for reducing posttraumatic stress disorder in female assault victims. *Journal of Consulting and Clinical Psychology, 67,* 194–200.

Foa, E. B., Rothbaum, B. O., Riggs, D., & Murdock, T. (1991). Treatment of post-traumatic stress disorder in rape victims: A comparison between cognitive-behavioral procedures and counseling. *Journal of Consulting and Clinical. Psychology, 59,* 715–723.

Lee, C., Gavriel, H., Drummond, P., Richards, J., & Greenwald, R. (2002). Treatment of PTSD: stress inoculation training with prolonged exposure compared to EMDR. *Journal of Clinical Psychology, 58,* 1071–1089.

Clinical Resources

Meichenbaum, D. (1985). *Stress inoculation training.* New York, NY: Pergamon Press.

Veronen, L. J., & Kilpatrick, D. G. (1983). Stress management for rape victims. In D. Meichenbaum & M. E. Jaremko (Eds.), *Stress reduction and prevention* (pp. 341–374). New York, NY: Plenum.

Workshop and Training Opportunities

National Center for PTSD
Dissemination and Training Division
VA Palo Alto Health Care System
Menlo Park, CA 94025
www.ptsd.va.gov/about/divisions/dissemination-training-division.asp

Behavioral Science Division (116B-2)
VA Boston Healthcare System
150 South Huntington Avenue
Boston, MA 02130
www.ptsd.va.gov/about/divisions/behavioral-science-division.asp

Women's Health Sciences Division (116B-3)
VA Boston Healthcare System
150 South Huntington Avenue
Boston, MA 02130
www.ptsd.va.gov/about/divisions/womens-health-sciences-division.asp

National Crime Victims Research and Treatment Center
Department of Psychiatry and Behavioral Sciences
Medical University of South Carolina
67 President Street, MSC 861
2nd Floor IOP South Building
Charleston, SC 29403
http://colleges.musc.edu/ncvc/

Bibliotherapy Resources

Chestman, K. R., Gilboa-Schectman, E., & Foa, E. (2008). *Prolonged Exposure therapy for PTSD* (teen workbook). New York, NY: Oxford University Press.

Foa, E., Hembree, E., & Rothbaum, B. (2007). *Prolonged exposure therapy for PTSD: Emotional processing of traumatic experiences* (client workbook). New York, NY: Oxford University Press.

Rosenbloom, D., & Williams, M. B. (2010). *Life after trauma: A workbook for healing* (2nd ed.). New York, NY: Guilford Press.

Rothbaum, B. O., Foa, E. B., & Hembree, E. (2007). *Reclaiming your life from a traumatic experience: Client Workbook.* New York, NY: Oxford University Press.

The International Society for Traumatic Stress Studies (ISTSS) provides numerous resources for professionals and victims of PTSD: www.istss.org/Home.htm.

The National Center for PTSD aims to help U.S. Veterans and others through research, education, and training on trauma and PTSD. It contains numerous public and professional resources and links to other resources: www.ptsd.va.gov.

Gift From Within is an international non-profit organization dedicated to those who suffer PTSD, those at risk for PTSD, and those who care for traumatized individuals. It develops and disseminates educational material, including videotapes, articles, books, and other resources through its Web site: www.giftfromwithin.org.

The Department of Veterans Affairs Bibliotherapy Resource Guide can be found online at: www.mirecc.va.gov/docs/VA_Bibliotherapy_Resource_Guide.pdf.

CHAPTER 5

How Do You Integrate Empirically Supported Treatments Into Treatment Planning?

Construction of an empirically informed treatment plan for posttraumatic stress disorder (PTSD) involves integrating objectives and treatment interventions consistent with identified empirically supported treatments (ESTs) into a client's treatment plan after you have determined that the client's primary problem fits those described in the target population of the EST research. Of course, implementing ESTs must be done in consideration of important client, therapist, and therapeutic relationship factors—consistent with the APA's definition of evidence-based practice.

Definitions

The behavioral definition statements describe *how the problem manifests itself in the client*. Although there are several common features of PTSD, the behavioral definition of PTSD for your client will be unique and specific to him or her. Your assessment will need to identify which features best characterize your client's presentation. Accordingly, the *behavioral definition* of your treatment plan is tailored to your individual client's clinical picture. When the primary problem reflects a recognized psychiatric diagnosis, the behavioral definition statements are usually closely aligned with diagnostic criteria such as those provided in the DSM or ICD. Examples of common PTSD definition statements are the following:

- Has been exposed to a traumatic event involving actual or perceived threat of death or serious injury
- Reports response of intense fear, helplessness, or horror to the traumatic event
- Experiences disturbing and persistent thoughts, images, and/or perceptions of the traumatic event
- Experiences frequent nightmares
- Describes a reliving of the event, particularly through dissociative flashbacks
- Displays significant psychological and/or physiological distress resulting from internal and external clues that are reminiscent of the traumatic event

- Intentionally avoids thoughts, feelings, or discussions related to the traumatic event
- Intentionally avoids activities, places, people, or objects (e.g., up-armored vehicles) that evoke memories of the event
- Is unable to remember various important aspects of the traumatic event
- Displays a significant decline in interest and engagement in activities
- Experiences feelings of detachment or distance from others
- Experiences an inability to experience loving feelings
- Reports a sense of a foreshortened future
- Experiences disturbances in sleep
- Experiences intense anger and irritability
- Reports difficulty concentrating, as well as feelings of sadness and guilt
- Reports hypervigilance
- Demonstrates an exaggerated startle response
- Engages in a pattern of substance abuse
- Acknowledges increased marital and family conflict
- Displays eruptions of occasional violence
- Displays social withdrawal, sadness, and thoughts of suicide
- Symptoms present more than one month
- Impairment in social, occupational, or other areas of functioning

You may select from the list of behavioral definitions of PTSD shown here. For example, with this disorder your client will obviously have a history of exposure to a traumatic stressor. Then there will be one or more symptoms from each of three symptom clusters: intrusive recollections, avoidant/numbing symptoms, and hyperarousal symptoms. You may include a symptom statement that is also commonly seen with PTSD but not part of the DSM criteria for the disorder. Examples include: "engages in a pattern of substance abuse" or "displays occasional eruptions of violence." Some statement about the duration of symptoms should be included, as well as a statement about the functional impairment caused by the disorder.

Goals

Goals are broad statements describing what you and the client would like the result of therapy to be. One statement may suffice, but more than one can be used in the treatment plan. Examples of common goal statements for PTSD are the following:

- Eliminates or reduces the negative impact trauma related symptoms have on social, occupational, and family functioning
- Returns to the level of psychological functioning prior to exposure to the traumatic event

- ➢ No longer experiences intrusive event recollections, avoidance of event reminders, intense arousal, or disinterest in activities or relationships
- ➢ Thinks about or openly discusses the traumatic event with others without experiencing psychological or physiological distress
- ➢ No longer avoids persons, places, activities, and objects that are reminiscent of the traumatic event
- ➢ Feels more relaxed and is less irritable and reactive

Objectives and Interventions

Objectives are statements that describe *small, observable steps the client must achieve* toward attaining the goal of successful treatment. Intervention statements describe the *actions taken by the therapist* to assist the client in achieving his/her objectives. Each objective must be paired with at least one intervention.

Assessment

All approaches to quality treatment start with a thorough assessment of the nature and history of the client's presenting problems. EST approaches rely on a thorough psychosocial assessment of the nature, history, and severity of the problem as experienced by the client.

Table 5.1 contains examples of assessment objectives and interventions for PTSD.

Table 5.1 Assessment Objectives and Interventions

Objectives	Interventions
1. Describe in detail the nature and history of the PTSD symptoms.	1. Establish rapport with the client toward building a therapeutic alliance. 2. Assess the type, frequency, intensity, duration, and history of the client's PTSD symptoms and their impact on functioning (e.g., *The Anxiety Disorders Interview Schedule for the DSM-IV* by DiNardo, Brown, & Barlow).
2. Cooperate with psychological testing.	1. Administer or refer for psychological testing or use objective measures to assess for the presence and severity of PTSD symptoms (e.g., MMPI-2, Impact of Events Scale, PTSD Symptom Scale, or Mississippi Scale for Combat Related PTSD); readminister as needed to assess outcome.
3. Acknowledge any substance use.	1. Assess the presence and degree of substance use by the client. 2. Refer the client for a comprehensive substance use evaluation and treatment, if necessary.
4. Verbalize the symptoms of depression, including any suicidal thoughts.	1. Assess the client's depth of depression and suicide potential and treat appropriately, taking the necessary safety precautions as indicated.

(*continued*)

Table 5.1 (Continued)

Objectives	Interventions
5. Describe the traumatic event in as much detail as comfort allows.	1. Gently and sensitively explore the client's recollection of the facts of the traumatic incident and their emotional reactions at the time.
6. Cooperate with a psychiatric evaluation to assess for the need for psychotropic medication.	1. Assess the client's need for medication (e.g., selective serotonin reuptake inhibitors) and arrange for prescription, if appropriate. 2. Monitor and evaluate the client's psychotropic medication prescription compliance and the effectiveness of the medication on his/her level of functioning.

Psychoeducation

A typical feature of many ESTs for PTSD is initial and ongoing psychoeducation. A common emphasis is helping the client learn about PTSD, the treatment, and its rationale. Often, books or other reading material are recommended to the client to supplement psychoeducation done in session. It is important to instill hope in the client and have him or her on board as a partner in the treatment process. Discussing the demonstrated efficacy of ESTs with the client can facilitate this.

Key Points

Common Emphases of Initial Psychoeducation

1. Teaching the client about the nature and etiology of the diagnosed condition
2. Informing the client regarding the various treatment options consistent with the best available evidence
3. Explaining the rationale for the treatment approach that will be used
4. Using reading assignments as homework, if needed, to facilitate understanding of psychoeducational goals

Table 5.2 contains examples of psychoeducational objectives and interventions for PTSD.

Table 5.2 Psychoeducational Objectives and Interventions

Objectives	Interventions
7. Verbalize an accurate understanding of PTSD and how it develops.	1. Discuss how PTSD results from exposure to trauma; results in intrusive recollection, unwarranted fears, anxiety, and a vulnerability to others' negative emotions, such as shame, anger, and guilt; and results in avoidance of thoughts, feelings, and activities associated with the trauma.

Objectives	Interventions
8. Verbalize an understanding of the treatment rationale for PTSD.	1. Educate the client about how effective treatments for PTSD help address the cognitive, emotional, and behavioral consequences of PTSD using cognitive and behavioral therapy approaches. 2. Assign the client to read psychoeducational chapters of books or treatment manuals on PTSD that explain its features, development, and treatment (e.g., *Overcoming Post-traumatic Stress Disorder* by Smyth or *Reclaiming Your Life from a Traumatic Experience: A Prolonged Exposure Treatment Program Workbook* by Rothbaum, Foa, & Hembree.)

Demonstration Vignette

PTSD Psychoeducation

Here we present the transcript of the dialogue depicted in the psychoeducation vignette.

Therapist: What brings you in for counseling today, Bonnie?

Client: It's been a rough several months for me. I'm not sleeping well. I have nightmares. I'm on edge and irritable. And sometimes I have flashbacks.

Therapist: I see. Your life has changed and you're struggling with tension, anxiety, and some bad memories. Can you tell me a little about what may have triggered all these problems?

Client: Well, I worked as a bank teller and the bank was robbed by a masked man with a big gun.

Therapist: I am sorry. I'm sure that was very frightening for you.

Client: It certainly was. I haven't been back there since it happened. I don't even drive down that street.

(*continued*)

Therapist: Okay. And how is it for you to talk about the robbery?

Client: I don't talk about it with anyone. It brings it all up again, but I know I'll have to here.

Therapist: I do need to learn some things about it; let's take it at your pace.

Client: Okay

Therapist: How long ago was the robbery?

Client: It's been about six or seven months ago, now.

Therapist: And was anyone threatened or injured during the incident?

Client: He shot the guard in the leg and he threatened to kill us all. He put the gun right to my friend Gail's head when she screamed. She was right next to me.

Therapist: Oh my. This had to be terribly scary for you and everyone else in the bank.

Client: It was.

Therapist: And since the robbery you've been experiencing several problems you didn't have before. You mentioned trouble sleeping, feeling more irritable, flashbacks. Can you tell me about the flashbacks?

Client: I'll just suddenly see some image from the incident, like Gail's face or the guard's leg.

Therapist: I see. And, of course, you've said that you haven't returned to work, or even gone near the bank. You've avoided driving on the same road. You've also avoided talking or thinking about the robbery?

Client: That's right. I try not to think about it, but sometimes it just jumps into my mind or something may remind me of it—like a TV commercial about a bank, or something like that. So I don't watch TV much anymore and I used to like doing that.

Therapist: So the thoughts force themselves into your mind at times. And how do you feel when that occurs?

Client: I get all nervous and tense again. Sometimes I get shaky and feel sick to my stomach. It's awful. I hate it.

Therapist: So it's almost like the robbery was happening all over again.

Client: Exactly.

Therapist: I can sense your frustration over this. What you are experiencing is Posttraumatic Stress Disorder, or PTSD. It's often seen in men and women in the military as they encounter life-threatening traumatic experiences on the battlefield. Your life-threatening experience occurred right here close to home, but your emotional, behavioral, and physical reaction is similar to our service men and women. PTSD is a type of anxiety disorder that is triggered by being a witness to or experiencing directly a traumatic event that brings on intense fear. PTSD often includes intrusive recollections of the trauma, like the flashbacks and nightmares you have been having.

Client: The nightmares are awful. They wake me up in a sweat.

Therapist: I know; unfortunately that's part of it. It's also common to feel upset, tense, or anxious or have trouble sleeping after experiencing such an intensely fearful event. And most people avoid things that remind them of the event, like thinking about it, talking about it, seeing things on TV that remind them of it—and in your case going back to the bank.

Client: That sounds like me.

Therapist: Yeah, you're experiencing PTSD and you have taken a big step today by seeking counseling to help you overcome it.

Client:	I have been thinking about coming here for a while and my husband has asked me over and over to get some help. Can this actually be treated?
Therapist:	Yes. There are approaches to treating PTSD that have been found to be very effective for many people. We'll talk about the options. I also have a book I would like you to read that explains more about PTSD and its treatment. I'll give it to you as you leave today. How does this sound to you, Bonnie?
Client:	Good. Thank you. I'm feeling a little relieved just hearing you talk about it. . . .

Critique of the Psychoeducation Demonstation Vignette

The following points were made in the critique:

a. This represents a session early in the assessment phase as the therapist gathers information about the trauma and its consequences.
b. The therapist used "I" messages to convey empathy and build rapport.
c. Both assessment and psychoeducation are occurring in this session, as the therapist clarifies the client's diagnosis and reassures her of treatment approaches that may help her.

Additional points that could be made:

a. The therapist reassures the client that the description of the traumatic incident will proceed at the client's pace.
b. The therapist clarifies and identifies how the symptoms have grown out of the trauma.

Comments you would like to make:

____

____

____

____

Homework: The homework exercise "How the Trauma Affects Me" (*Adult Psychotherapy Homework Planner*, 2nd ed., by Jongsma) is an example of an intervention consistent with assessment and psychoeducation. It is designed to help the client describe the symptoms that have been experienced, along with their frequency and severity (see www.wiley.com/go/PTSDwb).

Assessment/Psychoeducation Review

1. What are common emphases of initial psychoeducation?

Assessment/Psychoeducation Review Test Question

1. At what point in therapy is psychoeducation typically conducted?
   A. At the end of therapy
   B. During the assessment phase
   C. During the initial treatment session
   D. Throughout therapy

Prolonged Exposure

In prolonged exposure, the client recounts in detail the traumatic memory in the order in which the events unfolded, including his or her thoughts and feelings along the way. The client is essentially providing a running commentary on what he or she remembers happening. Typically, the therapist periodically asks for a rating of discomfort to assess the client's response and to get some indication of extinction. The process is repeated until the recounting no longer evokes high levels of distress, and until the trauma memories are experienced as memories rather than a re-living of the event.

Homework exercises in which the client does self-conducted imaginal exposure may be assigned after the client has made some progress and understands the procedure and its purpose.

There are several variations to exposing the client to the memory of the trauma. Examples of common methods of imaginal exposure include the following:

- Client verbally describes his or her experience with the traumatic stressor chronologically (commonly used in prolonged exposure therapy).
- Client writes and reads a narrative description his or her experience with the traumatic stressor (commonly used in cognitive processing therapy).
- Client listens to a recording of his or her description of the trauma (commonly used as an in- or between-session homework exercise in prolonged exposure and cognitive processing therapy).
- Client visualizes scenes associated with the trauma (commonly used in eye movement desensitization and reprocessing [EMDR], within the therapy's structured protocol).

Key Points

KEY FEATURES OF PROLONGED EXPOSURE

1. Ask the client to recall and describe the traumatic incident in as much detail as possible.
2. Include recollections of the thoughts and feelings experienced before, during, and after the incident.
3. Ask the client for a discomfort rating (e.g., a 0–10 SUDS rating) as the retelling progresses to gauge extinction.
4. Repeat the process until the discomfort is extinguished as reflected in the client ratings given.
5. Reach the goal of the incident being just a memory instead of a traumatic event that evokes overwhelming emotions and avoidance.

Table 5.3 contains examples of a objective and interventions consistent with prolonged exposure for PTSD.

Table 5.3 Projected Exposure Objective and Interventions

Objective	Interventions
9. Cooperate with trauma-focused prolonged exposure therapy.	1. Use prolonged exposure to process memories of the trauma, at a client-chosen level of detail, for an extended period of time (e.g., 60–90 minutes); repeat in future sessions until distress reduces and stabilizes (see *Prolonged Exposure Therapy for PTSD: Emotional Processing of Traumatic Experiences [Therapist Guide]* by Foa, Hembree, & Rothbaum; or *Posttraumatic Stress Disorder* by Resick & Calhoun). 2. Assign the client a homework exercise in which he or she does self-directed exposure to the memory of the trauma.

Demonstration Vignette

Prolonged Exposure

(*continued*)

Here we present the transcript of the dialogue depicted in the prolonged exposure vignette.

Therapist: As you know, Bonnie, our goal this session is to start talking about the robbery incident in a little more detail.

Client: Yeah, I know.

Therapist: I'm going to ask you to go through it as you remember it. You can tell me whatever you like. And if there are things you don't want to talk about, you don't have to. Okay?

Client: All right. Can I stop if I need to?

Therapist: Absolutely. Take this at your own pace. If you want a break, just stop. You can continue when you're ready. It may help to remind yourself, Bonnie, that you've been talking about this with me already, and you have been able to do it.

Client: If I get upset, I'll be okay. It'll pass?

Therapist: Perfect! You remembered your positive self-statements.

Client: Yeah.

Therapist: As you describe the incident, I'm going to periodically ask you to give me a quick SUDS rating. Just give me what you feel at that moment and continue on. Okay?

Client: Okay.

Therapist: Why don't we begin by getting comfortable, taking a few breaths, and relaxing a little bit . . . So what is your rating right now, Bonnie?

Client: About a 3 or 4. I'm a little nervous.

Therapist: Okay. You're fine. Nervousness is to be expected. Are you ready to begin or do you want to relax a little more?

Client: No, let's go ahead.

Therapist: Okay, good. So why don't you begin by telling me how your day began as you came to work that day?

Client: Well, I got to the bank at my usual time of 9:30. The other girls were arriving about the same time. Gail, who is the teller next to me, was a few minutes late because she was taking care of her sick daughter who was staying home from school. Gail was worried about her being home alone and almost didn't come in that day. She should've stayed home and she would have missed the robbery!

Therapist: Good, you're doing fine. Your rating?

Client: 5.

Therapist: Okay, go ahead and continue when you like.

Client: Well, the manager is always the one who unlocks the door at 10:00 A.M. The guard was over talking to Tom by his desk. Everything seemed normal. Nobody came in right away. But then this guy burst through the door with a mask on.

Therapist: Okay. What's your rating?

Client: 7.

Therapist: Okay. So this part is a little more provocative for you. That's understandable. You're doing okay?

Client: Yeah.

Therapist: Take your time, Bonnie. And remember, it's safe here. These are only images. Try to think of them like a motion picture. Do you want to continue or wait a little bit?

Client: No, it's okay . . . As soon as I saw him, I froze. He yelled, "Everybody put your hands high in the air!" and he showed us his gun. I remember that I started shaking, uncontrollably. I thought I was going to panic.

Therapist: That's understandable. It was a frightening situation to be in.

Client: It was. I'm shaking now a little just telling you about it.

Therapist: That's okay. Try to just let it be. You're doing fine. Again, they're just images. What's your rating right now?

Client: Still a 7.

Therapist: Okay. Take whatever time you need. Do you want to relax a little bit?

Client: Yeah. [Takes a few deep breaths]

Therapist: You can continue when you want.

Therapist: So, he backed up toward the door?

Client: Yeah, I could see his shoes, but I didn't want to look up too much.

Therapist: That was smart thinking.

Client: And then he ran out of the door. Everybody was kind of frozen. Tom ran over to the guard to see if he was okay. I saw that Gail was crying and shaking. I sat down next to her and I was shaking and crying too. We just hugged each other.

Therapist: I see. You helped comfort each other.

Client: Yeah, we just hugged each other.

Therapist: What's your rating, Bonnie?

Client: A 4.

Therapist: Okay, why don't we stop? Bonnie, you've done really well. I know this wasn't easy for you, but you made it through the whole thing.

Client: I didn't know if I could.

Therapist: I understand. That's anxiety making a false prediction again. You did make it through. You did a great job. Why don't we take a second to relax, and then we can talk about where we're going from here.

Critique of the Prolonged Exposure Demonstation Vignette

The following points were made in the critique:

a. The therapist does some cognitive restructuring and relaxation during administration of exposure.
b. More recent versions of exposure place less emphasis on relaxation. They encourage the client to stay with the feelings and allow them to gradually dissipate.

Additional points that could be made:

a. The therapist points out that the client has indeed been talking about the trauma already and has coped quite well.
b. The reassurance that the client is in a safe environment while talking about the trauma is helpful.

c. The therapist clearly and frequently notes and reinforces the client's success at coping while talking and thinking about the incident.

Comments you would like to make:

____

____

____

____

Homework: The homework exercise "Share the Painful Memory" (*Adult Psychotherapy Homework Planner*, 2nd ed., by Jongsma) focuses on allowing the client to describe the traumatic event in as much detail as is tolerable at the time of sharing. It is a step toward reliving the experience without being overwhelmed (see www.wiley.com/go/PTSDwb).

Prolonged Exposure Review

1. What are the various ways which imaginal exposure to the memory of the trauma can be conducted?
2. What are the key features of prolonged exposure?

Prolonged Exposure Review Test Question

1. Which of the following is a primary goal of prolonged exposure?
   A. A change from maladaptive to adaptive appraisals of the trauma experience
   B. Extinction of the emotional response to memories of the trauma
   C. Insight into the origin of the distress
   D. Unihibited expression of the distress associated with the trauma

Cognitive Therapy

Cognitive therapy is focused on identifying and changing maladaptive thoughts and beliefs that are related to the trauma or that have come about as a result of it. It typically involves teaching the client the connection between thoughts and feelings; identifying biases in the thoughts that may be perpetuating maladaptive emotional reactions like unwarranted fear and avoidance; challenging those thoughts and generating alternatives to them that correct for the biases; and finally engaging in behavioral experiments that test the predictions emanating from the alternative thoughts. Assumptions underlying the biased self-talk may also be examined, challenged, and changed.

Cognitive restructuring may be focused on trauma-related thoughts and feelings, on more present-day consequences, or both. When cognitive restructuring is focused on present-day issues, the biased and alternative thoughts may be used for prediction testing through behavioral experiments that resemble live exposure therapy, as discussed previously.

Key Points

Key Concepts in Cognitive Therapy

- Teaching the connection between thoughts and feelings
- Identifying biases in self-talk
- Generating alternative thoughts that correct for the biases
- Engaging in prediction testing of thoughts/beliefs through "behavioral experiments"
- Examining, challenging, and changing underlying assumptions

Cognitive therapy uses various techniques and strategies including psychoeducation, guided discovery, self-monitoring, Socratic questioning, rational disputation, role-playing, imagery, and behavioral experiments. It also uses interventions that derive from behavioral traditions such as teaching adaptive coping and problem-solving skills.

Key Points

Common Strategies and Techniques Used in Cognitive Therapy

- Psychoeducation
- Guided discovery
- Self-monitoring of thoughts, feelings, and actions
- Rational disputation of biased beliefs
- Socratic questioning
- Role-playing
- Imagery
- Behavioral experiments
- Teaching adaptive coping and problem-solving skills

Homework assignments are often used to strengthen cognitive restructuring done in session, and may involve journaling, exercises that reinforce positive changes, and those representing behavioral experiments.

Table 5.4 contains examples of a cognitive therapy objective and interventions for PTSD.

Table 5.4 Cognitive Therapy Objective and Interventions

Objective	Interventions
10. Identify, challenge, and replace biased, negative, and self-defeating thoughts resulting from the trauma.	1. Explore the client's schema and self-talk that mediate his/her trauma-related fears; identify and challenge biases; assist him/her in generating appraisals that correct for the biases and build confidence in them. 2. Assign the client to keep a daily log of automatic thoughts associated with themes of threat and danger (e.g., "Negative Thoughts Trigger Negative Feelings" in the *Adult Psychotherapy Homework Planner,* 2nd ed., by Jongsma); process the journal material to challenge distorted thinking patterns with reality-based thoughts and to generate predictions for behavioral experiments. 3. Reinforce the client's positive cognitions that foster a sense of safety and security and decrease fearful and avoidance behavior (see "Positive Self-Talk" in the *Adult Psychotherapy Homework Planner,* 2nd ed., by Jongsma). 4. Assign the client a homework exercise in which he/she identifies fearful self-talk, tests (through behavioral experiments) the predictions from these dysfunctional thoughts, and creates reality-based alternatives; review and reinforce success, providing corrective feedback for failure (e.g., *Overcoming Post-traumatic Stress Disorder* by Smyth).

Demonstration Vignette

Cognitive Therapy

Here we present the transcript of the dialogue depicted in the cognitive therapy vignette.

Therapist: Bonnie, today I'd like to continue to focus on how the PTSD is affecting your thinking patterns. Are you okay with that?

Client: I guess so. Sure. Is this about that material you asked me to read . . . about the ways thinking can trigger anxiety?

Therapist: Exactly. We've talked about how thinking influences our emotional reactions to things. And we've talked about how to listen to your self-talk. PTSD can introduce changes in the way that we think about things, and those thoughts can create the negative emotional reactions associated with it. This pattern then makes people want to avoid thinking about it at all because the feelings that are triggered are so distressing.

Client: Yeah. I read about "biased thought patterns" and remember something about "catastrophizing" or something like that. Right?

Therapist: Yes, that's one that we will be exploring. Very good. And there's one called "filtering," and "black or white thinking," and "discounting," and several others. Let's look at your thoughts about the bank robbery and see if there are any of these biases that may be causing you to stay fearful and avoid reminders of the robbery.

Client: Okay.

Therapist: Since our last session, you got a chance to record some of your self-talk around this issue?

Client: Yeah. I put some of my thoughts down about it.

Therapist: What did you find?

Client: Well, I wrote that, "If I think about it or talk about it, I'm going to get upset." And I wrote, "I'm afraid I'm going to fall apart just like I did when the guy finally ran out of the bank." I fell to the floor, shaking and crying. I couldn't help it. It was awful.

Therapist: I know this isn't easy, and I appreciate that you're trying. You've done a very good job of capturing the kind of self-talk we want to become aware of. Now can you see that this self-talk is predicting that if you think about the incident, you'll experience the same emotions you did when the robbery actually occurred, and that you'll fall apart if you do. Can you think of that as a prediction?

Client: Okay. Yeah.

Therapist: And when you're thinking these thoughts, it makes you feel how?

Client: Scared.

Therapist: Yes, it would anyone. And anyone's tendency at that time would be to avoid thinking about it. Wouldn't it?

Client: Yeah, which is what I do.

Therapist: Exactly. So, let's examine whether this prediction is actually true, and if not, let's see if we can identify how it's biased. You did actually shake and cry after the real incident, something we'd all agree is a normal reaction. But this prediction, the one I want to focus on, is that talking or thinking about the incident will make you break down just like when it really happened. Do you agree?

Client: Yes, that's true.

Therapist: And although you've been trying to avoid it, you actually have talked about it several times, with me. So, let's be very accurate here. What have you felt when talking about the incident to me?

(continued)

Client:	I don't know. I guess nervous at first. I was afraid to, but I did. It still scares me to think about it, but I've been able to do it here.
Therapist:	Yes, you have. That's being very accurate. And that's not the outcome that the prediction is making, "If I talk about it, it's going to get worse, I'm going to break down." In fact, you've been nervous and scared to a degree, but you've been able to do it. You haven't broken down. But do you see how the self-talk isn't quite accurate about what's going to happen when you think or talk about the robbery; the prediction is wrong?
Client:	Yeah. I hadn't really thought about that. I guess I have talked about it with you. It's not been easy though.
Therapist:	I understand. It's not easy, but it is something you've been able to do.
Client:	That's true.
Therapist:	So, Bonnie, this prediction that if you think or talk about the incident your feelings will overwhelm you and you will lose control and break down. It hasn't been happening that way. In reality—it hasn't been easy, but it has been manageable. So what bias from our list might be operating in this fearful prediction?
Client:	That's catastrophizing, isn't it?
Therapist:	Yes it is. Catastrophizing is a common consequence of having experienced a trauma. After something like that, there's a tendency to overestimate the likelihood that the worst-case scenarios are going to happen. When we're catastrophizing we're also discounting our ability to cope with and recover from experiencing the feelings associated with the trauma. When you think that recalling the robbery will result in such drastic consequences, it makes your fear of talking about it escalate and your desire to avoid it stronger.
Client:	I understand, but what do I do about it?
Therapist:	As a first step, why don't you try replacing the thought of "I'm going to lose control" with something more accurate, like, "Even if I cry and shake, it will pass. I can pull myself together. I can face these memories in small steps."
Client:	Tell myself: "Even if I cry or shake, I can handle it. I can face this stuff in small steps?"
Therapist:	That thought is more accurate. It also counters the part of catastrophizing that forgets that you can cope.

Critique of the Cognitive Therapy Demonstration Vignette

The following points were made in the critique:

a. The therapist challenges the client's biased thought patterns with evidence of the client's ability to talk and think about the trauma without breaking down.
b. Predictions need to be repeatedly formulated from the biased thoughts and then tested against reality to convince the client that the biases are inaccurate and allow her to discover alternate positive messages.

Additional points that could be made:

a. The therapist is teaching the client how biased thought patterns such as catastrophizing influence her feelings and behavior. Psychoeducation is used throughout the process.

b. The therapist draws out and clarifies the client's central biased thought that she will experience the same debilitating emotions as when the trauma occurred and then break down if she talks or even thinks about the trauma.

Comments you would like to make:

____

____

____

____

Homework: The exercise "Negative Thoughts Trigger Negative Feelings" (*Adult Psychotherapy Homework Planner*, 2nd ed., by Jongsma) is an example of an intervention that is consistent with cognitive therapy and is designed to help educate the client about biased thinking and its impact on emotions. This assignment also provides opportunity for the client to examine her thinking in response to events in her life and begin to develop positive, reality-based replacement thoughts. Additional homework exercises consistent with cognitive restructuring are "Positive Self Talk," "Journal and Replace Self-Defeating Thoughts," and "Journal of Distorted, Negative Thoughts" (see www.wiley.com/go/ptsdwb).

Cognitive Therapy Review

1. What are key concepts in cognitive therapy?

2. What strategies and techniques are commonly used in cognitive therapy?

Cognitive Therapy Review Test Question

1. In cognitive therapy, clients are often asked to test the validity of biased fearful thoughts and beliefs against alternatives that correct for the bias. This is often done by converting the thoughts into predictions and then testing them through "real-life" exercises to see which prediction is best supported. These exercises are called:

   A. Behavioral experiments
   B. Conflict-resolution
   C. Exposure exercises
   D. Problem-solving

Cognitive Processing Therapy

Cognitive processing therapy (CPT) is an empirically supported treatment for PTSD designed to challenge and change biased beliefs and self-blame. Socratic questioning is a common technique of the therapy. CPT also contains an exposure component involving writing about the traumatic event. The primary goal of therapy is to modify beliefs about the meaning and implications of the traumatic event.

As an aid to understanding this therapy, the following is presented as a typical progression of therapeutic activities in CPT (note: this section is not on the DVD):

- Educate about PTSD; overview the treatment; provide a rationale for the treatment.
- Assign the client to write a description of the meaning of the traumatic event (i.e., the impact statement).
- Ask the client to read and discuss the impact statement.
- Teach the client the relationship between thoughts, behaviors, and emotions associated with the trauma.
- Ask the client to write a detailed description of the traumatic event; ask the client to read the description daily.
- In session, ask the client to read the statement; use cognitive therapy techniques to question biased thoughts and beliefs.
- Repeat this process with increasing emphasis on teaching the client to challenge biased cognitions and understanding the relationship between thoughts, emotions, and behaviors.
- Ask the client again to write a description of the event, but now reflecting new thoughts and beliefs; ask the client to read and discuss this restructured version of the event.

Key Points

Key Elements of Cognitive Processing Therapy

- Cognitive restructuring of thoughts and beliefs related to the trauma (its impact on the client)
- Trauma-focused imaginal exposure to a narrative description of the trauma written and read by the client
- Cognitive restructuring of the thoughts and feelings elicited by exposure to the trauma memory

Table 5.5 Cognitive Processing Therapy Objective and Interventions

Objective	Interventions
11. Write and read a narrative account of the trauma while examining thoughts and feelings associated with it.	1. Use cognitive processing therapy techniques that ask the client to write and then read a narrative account of the traumatic incident while cognitively restructuring biased, maladaptive thoughts and feelings associated with it. 2. Assign homework in which the client listens to a recording of the narrative read during the preceding session; review during subsequent session; process thoughts and feelings associated with it.

Table 5.5 above contains examples of an objective and interventions reflective of cognitive processing therapy for PTSD. Objectives and interventions previously discussed for cognitive therapy (see Table 5.4) also apply to cognitive processing therapy and would be included in your treatment plan.

Homework: Homework exercises consistent with cognitive restructuring are "Positive Self-Talk," "Journal and Replace Self-Defeating Thoughts," and "Journal of Distorted, Negative Thoughts" (see www.wiley.com/go/ptsdwb).

Cognitive Processing Therapy Review

1. What are the key elements of cognitive processing therapy?

Cognitive Processing Therapy Review Test Question

1. Which of the following homework exercises is most consistent with cognitive processing therapy (CPT)?
   A. Doing a relaxation exercise
   B. Doing an exposure to a currently feared situation
   C. Listening to an audiotaped description of the traumatic event
   D. Participating in a pleasurable activity

Live Exposure/Exposure *in vivo*

In present-focused treatments for PTSD, live exposure, or exposure *in vivo*, is commonly used. Exposure is to objects, situations, and/or activities that are associated with the trauma and often feared and avoided. These exposures are to safe situations, but ones that elicit maladaptive emotional, physical, cognitive, and behavioral reactions in the client due to their association with the trauma. Examples include driving a car again after being involved in an accident or using elevators again after having been assaulted in an elevator. Exposure is designed to help the client realize that the feared situation is no longer dangerous and that the anxiety associated with it does not persist when the client performs the feared activity repeatedly. A fear hierarchy in which situations are identified, rated, and then ranked from least to most feared typically guides exposure. Therapeutic sessions and homework assignments involving graduated exposure characterize the intervention.

Key Points

Key Elements of Live Exposure or Exposure *in vivo*

- In present-focused treatments for PTSD, live exposure, or exposure *in vivo*, is commonly used.
- Exposure is to objects, situations, and/or activities that are associated with the trauma and often feared and avoided.
- A fear hierarchy in which situations are identified, rated, and then ranked from least to most feared typically guides exposure.
- Therapeutic sessions and homework assignments involving graduated exposure characterize the treatment.
- Exposure is designed to help the client realize that the feared situation is no longer dangerous and that the anxiety associated with it does not persist when he or she performs the feared activity repeatedly.

Homework: "Gradually Reducing Your Phobic Fear" (*Adult Psychotherapy Homework Planner,* 2nd ed. by Jongsma) is an exercise that leads the client through an exposure trial and asks the client to record his or her responses (see www.wiley.com/go/ptsdwb).

Table 5.6 contains examples of an objective and interventions reflective of live exposure/exposure *in vivo.*

Table 5.6 Live Exposure/Exposure *in vivo* Objective and Interventions

Objective	Interventions
12. Participate in present-focused exposure therapy involving safe, but currently feared activities.	1. Direct and assist the client in constructing a fear and avoidance hierarchy of trauma-related stimuli. 2. Use *in vivo* exposure in which the client gradually exposes him- or herself to objects, situations, places negatively associated with the trauma. 3. Assign the client a homework exercise in which he/she does an exposure exercise and records responses (see "Gradually Reducing Your Phobic Fear" in the *Adult Psychotherapy Homework Planner,* 2nd ed., by Jongsma, or *Overcoming Post-traumatic Stress Disorder* by Smyth); review and reinforce progress; problem-solve obstacles.

Live Exposure Review

1. What is exposure designed to accomplish?

Live Exposure Review Test Question

1. Which of the following therapeutic assignments is most consistent with exposure *in vivo*?
   A. Listen to a narrative account of the traumatic experience, and record thoughts and feelings.
   B. Write a description of the traumatic experience, include associated thoughts and feelings.
   C. Watch a film unrelated to the trauma, that you enjoy.
   D. Visit a site that is safe, but similar to one associated with the trauma.

Stress Inoculation Training

Stress inoculation training, or SIT, is a flexible, multicomponent, present-focused therapy that is tailored to the individual client's needs. It is focused on improving the client's current adaptive functioning, as opposed to focusing on the trauma itself. SIT begins with a thorough assessment of the client's problems, strengths, deficits, and environment. Interventions typically include psychoeducation, calming and coping skills training (e.g., relaxation training and coping self-statements), personal and interpersonal skills training (e.g., communication and problem-solving skills), cognitive interventions (e.g., guided self-dialogue), and, in the case of anxiety-based

Key Points

KEY ELEMENTS OF STRESS INOCULATION TRAINING

- Psychoeducation
- Calming and coping skills training
- Personal and interpersonal skills building
- Cognitive interventions (e.g., guided self-dialogue)
- Imaginal and/or live present-focused exposure

Key Points

COMMON STRATEGIES AND TECHNIQUES OF STRESS INOCULATION TRAINING

- Instruction
- Modeling
- Covert (or imaginal) modeling
- Role-playing
- Positive reinforcement

problems, exposure to what is feared and often avoided. SIT uses several techniques typical of cognitive and behavior therapies such as instruction, modeling and covert (or imaginal) modeling, role-playing, and positive reinforcement to teach skills.

Table 5.7 contains examples of objectives and interventions consistent with stress inoculation training for PTSD. Objectives and interventions previously discussed for cognitive therapy (Table 5.4) and live exposure (Table 5.6) may also apply to a treatment plan describing the use stress inoculation training for PTSD and would be included should you decide to use them as well.

Table 5.7 Stress Inoculation Training Objectives and Interventions

Objectives	Interventions
13. Learn and implement calming and coping strategies to manage challenging situations related to trauma.	1. Teach the client strategies from stress inoculation training, such as relaxation, breathing control, covert modeling (i.e., imagining the successful use of the strategies) and/or role-playing for managing fears until a sense of mastery is evident (see *Clinical Handbook for Treating PTSD* by Meichenbaum).
14. Learn and implement guided self-dialogue to manage thoughts, feelings, and urges brought on by encounters with trauma-related situations.	1. Teach the client a guided self-dialogue procedure in which he/she learns to recognize maladaptive self-talk, challenges its biases, copes with engendered feelings, overcomes avoidance, and reinforces his/her accomplishments; review and reinforce progress; problem-solve obstacles.

Demonstration Vignette

Guided Self-Dialogue

Here we present the transcript of the dialogue depicted in the guided self-dialogue therapy vignette.

Therapist: So, let's talk about an approach we want to try that's designed to help you with the goal of doing things that you've been avoiding. It's called guided self-dialogue.

Client: Okay. How do you do it?

Therapist: Well, we're going to break any task into four steps. With each step we're going to identify self-talk and any coping strategies we want to use to help us manage it. Let's use this sheet. It helps take us through each of the steps. Then we can apply it to a real task.

So, the four steps are: (1) preparing for the activity, (2) managing the demands of the activity, (3) managing your own feelings during the activity, and (4) looking at it afterward, recognizing how you did—building upon it.

Client: So these are examples of the things I might want to ask myself or say to myself?

Therapist: Yes, before any activity. Let's look at these and see if you feel any apply. We may come up with a few of our own too. So under *preparing for the activity*, you want to ask yourself: "What exactly is it I have to do?" We want to be very specific and break it down into steps. Then, "What exactly am I afraid of?" Again, we want to be very specific and challenge the fear with these questions: First, "What is the true likelihood of it actually happening the way I'm picturing it?" Here we want to be as objective as possible, like we've been doing. And if it's not likely, we want to let it go and think about what actually is likely. But if what we are afraid of could happen, we want to ask, "How bad would it really be if it happened, and how would I want to cope?"

Therapist: Okay Bonnie, under *preparing for the activity*, one of your fears is that while you are driving by the bank you're going to panic and do something out of control like have a wreck or just stop. And to the question, "What is the actual probability of that happening?" You said, "Not likely."

Client: Well, I might panic, but it's probably not likely that I'll lose control—at least when I think of it objectively. I'm still nervous about it.

Therapist: Nervous that . . . ?

Client: I won't handle it well.

Therapist: That's understandable. It brings us to the next one: "How bad would it actually be if you got nervous or even panicked. And, what would you want to try to do?"

Client: Well, I wouldn't like it, but I guess I would just pull over if it got bad—until I could calm down.

Therapist: That's an option. And the self-talk might be, "If I get too nervous, I'll just pull over and calm myself down until I can go again."

Client: Yeah.

Therapist: You may find that panicking isn't the most likely thing, but does it feel better to have a plan for it?

Client: Yeah. I'd rather be prepared.

Therapist: I understand. So, let's imagine you did panic and felt you had to pull over. How would you want to try to calm yourself?

Client: Just breathe and relax, like we've done.

Therapist: And what would you try to do with your thoughts?

Client: Just talk to myself, try to build my self-confidence.

Therapist: Saying what? What helps you regroup and get back to what you are trying to do?

Client: Probably something like, "It's just your heart racing. You can do this." Things like that.

Therapist: I think that's excellent. So we have a plan for dealing with nervousness if it gets too uncomfortable. Do you think you will need it, or do you think driving by anxiously perhaps is more likely?

(*continued*)

Client: Actually, just talking about doing it and thinking of how and stuff is making me feel like I can probably do this.

Therapist: Okay, so let's go through each question you answered, put this activity together, and the self-dialogue you came up with. Then we can rehearse doing the whole thing in imagination.

Client: Okay.

Therapist: So our situation is driving by the bank. Under the question, "What am I afraid of?" you said panicking and losing control, possibly having an accident. When we asked about the actual probability, your answer translates to something like this: "Panicking isn't likely. If it happens, it's not likely to overwhelm me, make me lose control, and cause an accident. I may get nervous, but I can handle that." Do you want to keep these or modify them in any way?

Client: That sounds good. I may want to say, "If it happens, it's not going to overwhelm me" instead of "it's not likely to," too.

Therapist: Okay, good. That helps more?

Client: Yeah. It makes me feel stronger.

Therapist: Okay, good. Next, when we explored the question, "How will I manage my feelings while I am driving?" we came up with, "I'll stay focused on what I'm doing, use my breathing to relax. It's just my heart beating faster. I can do this." Do you want to use that, or modify it in any way?

Client: No, I think that will help me. Maybe we could add, "It will go away when I get through this."

Therapist: Okay. And finally we looked at the unlikely worst case and ask, "If I do get to feeling too nervous, what will I do?" That came out as, "If I need to, I can always just pull over and calm down before starting back again." How does that sound?

Client: Good.

Therapist: So let's put all these pieces together and rehearse using them to accomplish driving by the bank.

Client: Okay.

Critique of the Guided Self-Dialogue Demonstration Vignette

The following points were made in the critique:

a. Guided self-dialogue is a combination of many techniques and skills training in a consolidated approach to managing stress.
b. Guided self-dialogue grows out of stress inoculation training, as it gives the client tools to manage anticipated stressful events.

Additional points that could be made:

a. The therapist draws out from the client alternative positive self-talk to replace dysfunctional, biased thoughts, and then writes down the more positive self-talk.

b. The client shows progress with her cognitive restructuring skills when she spontaneously puts forth an even stronger, more confident self-talk statement about her ability to cope with stress of driving by the bank.

Comments you would like to make:

____

____

____

____

Homework: The exercise "Analyze the Probability of a Feared Event" (*Adult Psychotherapy Homework Planner*, 2nd ed., by Jongsma) is an example of an intervention that can be used to aid the guided self-dialogue process. This assignment provides an opportunity for the client to examine both his/her fears and the self-talk messages that support those fears. Additional homework exercises consistent with cognitive restructuring are "Positive Self-Talk," "Journal and Replace Self-Defeating Thoughts," and "Journal of Distorted, Negative Thoughts." "Replacing Fears with Positive Messages" is another homework assignment that helps clients identify their maladaptive cognitions and replace them with positive alternatives (see www.wiley.com/go/ptsdwb).

Stress Inoculation Training Review

1. How would you describe stress inoculation training for PTSD?

Stress Inoculation Training Review Test Question

1. Which of the following best describes the goal of stress inoculation training (SIT)?

   A. Improving a client's adaptation to the current environment
   B. Improving a client's calming skills
   C. Improving a client's cognitive coping skills
   D. Improving a client's communication skills

Eye Movement Desensitization and Reprocessing

Eye movement desensitization and reprocessing (EMDR) uses exposure to images of the trauma with concurrent eye movement in a highly structured protocol. The classic EMDR procedure asks clients to hold an image related to the trauma in their mind's eye while tracking an object back and forth across their visual field, usually the therapist's fingers. The client is asked to monitor this image as well as thoughts, emotions, and physical sensations associated with it while they engage in the eye movement task. If no change is detected in any of those domains during the task, the task is repeated. If change is detected in any of them, the client then holds this new experience, whatever it is, and repeats the procedure. The procedure is repeated in this way until a therapeutic change is achieved in which the image, thoughts, feelings, or all of these change in a way that is less threatening and more reassuring to the client. Then, this new perspective is reinforced by holding it while doing the eye movement procedure. Other images are subjected to the same process until the change has generalized across various images related to the trauma.

Key Points

Summary of the EMDR Protocol Elements

1. The client is asked to monitor an image associated with the trauma as well as thoughts, emotions, and physical sensations associated with it while they engage in the eye movement task.
2. If no change is detected in any of those domains during the task, the task is repeated.
3. If change is detected in any of the domains, the client then holds this new experience, whatever it is, and repeats the procedure.
4. The procedure is repeated in this way until a therapeutic change is achieved.
5. This new perspective is reinforced by holding it while doing the eye movement procedure.
6. Other images are subjected to the same process until the change has generalized across various images related to the trauma.

Table 5.8 contains an example of an EMDR objective and intervention for PTSD. In a highly structured, identifiable protocol such as this, the treatment plan need only name it.

Table 5.8 EMDR Objective and Intervention

Objective	Intervention
15. Participate in eye movement desensitization and reprocessing (EMDR) to reduce emotional reaction to the traumatic event.	1. Use eye movement desensitization and reprocessing (EMDR) to reduce the client's emotional reactivity to the traumatic event and reduce PTSD symptoms.

Eye Movement Desensitization and Reprocessing Review

1. What are the key elements of an EMDR protocol?

Eye Movement Desensitization and Reprocessing Review Test Question

1. EMDR is a trauma-focused intervention. Through what primary therapeutic technique does the treatment desensitize clients to memories of the trauma?
   A. Repeated exposure to images associated with the trauma
   B. Repeated pairing of relaxation with images of the trauma
   C. Repeated reading of a description of the trauma experience
   D. Repeated describing by the client of the trauma experience

Chapter Reference

Jongsma, A. E. (2006). *Adult psychotherapy homework planner* (2nd ed.). Hoboken, NJ: Wiley.

CHAPTER 6

What Are Considerations for Relapse Prevention?

Whether treated pharmacologically, psychologically, or both, posttraumatic stress disorder (PTSD) can relapse. Let's take a look at some common considerations in relapse prevention interventions and how they can be incorporated into your treatment plan.

1. Provide a rationale for relapse prevention that discusses the risk and introduces strategies for preventing it.
   - One of the first steps in relapse prevention interventions is to provide a *rationale* for them. This typically involves a discussion of the risk for relapse and how using the relapse prevention approach we will outline can lower that risk.

2. Discuss with the client the distinction between a lapse and relapse, associating a lapse with a temporary setback and relapse with a return to a sustained pattern of depressive thinking, feeling, interpersonal withdrawal, and/or avoidance.
   - A lapse is presented as a rather common, temporary setback that may involve, for example, re-experiencing an intrusive recollection of the trauma or finding oneself avoiding something safe associated with the trauma after having not had such a recollection for some time.
   - Relapse, on the other hand, is described as a return to a sustained pattern of thinking, feeling, and acting that is characteristic of PTSD.
   - The rationale for this distinction is that lapses do not need to develop into a relapse if they can be caught and managed.

3. Identify and rehearse managing high-risk situations for a lapse.
   - High-risk situations that might make the client vulnerable to a lapse are identified. This discussion may be informed by past "difficult" experiences or anticipated new ones. Some examples include:
     - Having an interpersonal conflict after having not had one for some time

- ➢ Going to a new place where exposure hasn't been done, and being in the presence of old triggers for it
- ➢ Having a stressful day, week, or other period and starting to ruminate negatively about the trauma

➢ For the high-risk situations identified, the therapist leads the client in a rehearsal of using skills learned in therapy to manage them, including the skills of developing a tolerance for the lapse while working on how to begin problem-solving them.

4. Instruct the client to routinely use strategies learned in therapy, building them into his/her life as much as possible.
   ➢ In addition to using skills learned in therapy to manage high-risk situations, clients are also encouraged to use strategies learned in therapy during their day-to-day life. Examples include everyday exposures, self-statements reflecting the new messages gained through cognitive restructuring, and problem-solving.

5. Develop a coping card on which coping strategies and other important information can be kept.
   ➢ Sometimes clients benefit from having a coping card or some other reminder of important strategies and information regarding relapse prevention.

6. Schedule periodic maintenance or "booster" sessions to help the client maintain therapeutic gains and problem-solve challenges.
   ➢ Periodic "booster" sessions of therapy can help reinforce positive changes, problem-solve challenges, and facilitate continued improvement, so clients are invited to periodically revisit therapy for these purposes.

Common Considerations in Relapse Prevention

1. Explain the rationale of relapse prevention interventions
2. Distinguish between lapse and relapse
3. Identify and rehearse managing high-risk situations for a lapse
4. Encourage routine use of skills learned in therapy
5. Consider developing a coping card
6. Schedule periodic "booster" therapy sessions

Table 6.1 contains examples of how common considerations in relapse prevention could be incorporated into a psychotherapy treatment plan.

Table 6.1 Integrating Relapse Prevention Objective and Interventions into the Treatment Plan

Objective	Interventions
1. Learn and implement strategies to prevent relapse of posttraumatic stress disorder.	1. Provide a rationale for relapse prevention that discusses the risk and introduces strategies for preventing it. 2. Discuss with the client the distinction between a lapse and relapse, associating a lapse with a temporary setback and relapse with a return to a sustained pattern of thinking, feeling, and behaving that is characteristic of PTSD. 3. Identify and rehearse the management of future situations or circumstances in which lapses could occur. 4. Instruct the client to routinely use strategies learned in therapy (e.g., continued everyday exposure, cognitive restructuring, problem-solving), building them into his/her life as much as possible. 5. Develop a coping card on which coping strategies and other important information can be kept (e.g., guidelines for exposure, positive coping statements, other reminders that were helpful to the client during therapy). 6. Schedule periodic maintenance or "booster" sessions to help the client maintain therapeutic gains and problem-solve challenges.

Chapter Review

1. What are the common considerations in relapse prevention?

Chapter Review Test Question

1. James is nearing the end of his treatment for PTSD. For several weeks he has successfully been completing exposures to situations associated with the trauma. His therapist gives him a homework assignment that asks him to list future situations that might challenge him to revert back to his old fearful and avoidant way of coping. They plan to review the list and develop a plan for managing the challenges effectively. Which consideration in relapse prevention is depicted in this example?

   A. Developing a coping card
   B. Distinguishing between lapse and relapse
   C. Encouraging routine use of skills learned in therapy
   D. Identifying high-risk situations for a lapse

Closing Remarks and Resources

As we note on the DVD, it is important to be aware that the research support for any particular EST supports the identified treatment as it was delivered in the empirical studies. The use of only selected objectives or interventions from ESTs may not be empirically supported.

If you want to incorporate an EST into your treatment plan, it should reflect the major objectives and interventions of the approach. Note that in addition to their primary objectives and interventions, many ESTs have options within them that may or may not be used depending on the client's need (e.g., skills training). Most treatment manuals, books, and other training programs identify the primary objectives and interventions used in the EST.

An existing resource for integrating research-supported treatments into treatment planning is the Practice*Planners*® Series[1] of treatment planners. The series contains several books that have integrated goals, objectives, and interventions consistent with those of identified ESTs into treatment plans for several applicable problems and disorders:

- *The Severe and Persistent Mental Illness Treatment Planner* (Berghuis, Jongsma, & Bruce)
- *The Family Therapy Treatment Planner* (Dattilio, Jongsma, & Davis)
- *The Complete Adult Psychotherapy Treatment Planner* (Jongsma, Peterson, & Bruce)
- *The Adolescent Psychotherapy Treatment Planner* (Jongsma, Peterson, McInnis, & Bruce)
- *The Child Psychotherapy Treatment Planner* (Jongsma, Peterson, McInnis, & Bruce)
- *The Veterans and Active Duty Military Psychotherapy Treatment Planner* (Moore & Jongsma)
- *The Addiction Treatment Planner* (Perkinson, Jongsma, & Bruce)
- *The Couples Psychotherapy Treatment Planner* (O'Leary, Heyman, & Jongsma)
- *The Older Adult Psychotherapy Treatment Planner* (Frazer, Hinrichsen, & Jongsma).

Finally, it is important to remember that the purpose of this series is to demonstrate the process of evidence-based psychotherapy treatment planning for common mental health problems. It is designed to be informational in nature, and does not intend to be a substitute for clinical training in the interventions discussed and demonstrated. In accordance with ethical guidelines, therapists should have competency in the services they deliver.

---

[1]These books are updated frequently; please check with the publisher for the latest editions and for further information about the Practice*Planners*® series.

APPENDIX **A**

A Sample Evidence-Based Treatment Plan for Posttraumatic Stress Disorder

Primary Problem: Posttraumatic Stress Disorder (PTSD)

Behavioral Definitions:

1. Has been exposed to a traumatic event involving actual or perceived threat of death or serious injury.
2. Reports response of intense fear, helplessness, or horror to the traumatic event.
3. Experiences disturbing and persistent thoughts, images, and/or perceptions of the traumatic event.
4. Experiences frequent nightmares.
5. Describes a reliving of the event, particularly through dissociative flashbacks.
6. Displays significant psychological and/or physiological distress resulting from internal and external clues that are reminiscent of the traumatic event.
7. Intentionally avoids thoughts, feelings, or discussions related to the traumatic event.
8. Intentionally avoids activities, places, people, or objects (e.g., up-armored vehicles) that evoke memories of the event.
9. Displays a significant decline in interest and engagement in activities.
10. Experiences disturbances in sleep.
11. Reports difficulty concentrating as well as feelings of guilt.
12. Reports hypervigilance
13. Demonstrates an exaggerated startle response.
14. Symptoms present more than one month.
15. Impairment in social, occupational, or other areas of functioning.

Diagnosis: Posttraumatic Stress Disorder, Chronic (309.81)

Long-Term Goals:

1. Eliminates or reduces the negative impact trauma-related symptoms have on social, occupational, and family functioning.
2. Returns to the level of psychological functioning prior to exposure to the traumatic event.
3. No longer experiences intrusive event recollections, avoidance of event reminders, intense arousal, or disinterest in activities or relationships.
4. Can think about or openly discuss the traumatic event with others without experiencing psychological or physiological distress.
5. No longer avoids persons, places, activities, and objects that are reminiscent of the traumatic event.

Objectives	Interventions
1. Describe in detail the nature and history of the PTSD symptoms.	1. Establish rapport with the client toward building a therapeutic alliance. 2. Assess the type, frequency, intensity, duration, and history of the client's PTSD symptoms and their impact on functioning (e.g., *The Anxiety Disorders Interview Schedule for the DSM-IV* by DiNardo, Brown, & Barlow).
2. Cooperate with psychological testing.	1. Administer or refer for psychological testing, or use objective measures to assess for the presence and severity of PTSD symptoms (e.g., *MMPI-2, Impact of Events Scale, PTSD Symptom Scale, or Mississippi Scale for Combat-Related PTSD*); readminister as needed to assess outcome.
3. Acknowledge any substance use.	1. Assess the presence and degree of substance use by the client. 2. Refer the client for a comprehensive substance use evaluation and treatment, if necessary.
4. Verbalize any symptoms of depression, including any suicidal thoughts.	1. Assess the client's depth of depression and suicide potential and treat appropriately, taking the necessary safety precautions as indicated.
5. Describe the traumatic event in as much detail as comfort allows.	1. Gently and sensitively explore the client's recollection of the facts of the traumatic incident and his or her cognitive and emotional reactions at the time.
6. Cooperate with a psychiatric evaluation to assess for the need for psychotropic medication.	1. Assess the client's need for medication (e.g., selective serotonin reuptake inhibitors) and arrange for prescription, if appropriate. 2. Monitor and evaluate the client's psychotropic medication prescription compliance and the effectiveness of the medication on his/her level of functioning.
7. Verbalize an accurate understanding of PTSD and how it develops.	1. Discuss how PTSD results from exposure to trauma; results in intrusive recollection, unwarranted fears, anxiety, and a vulnerability to others' negative emotions (such as shame, anger, and guilt); and results in avoidance of thoughts, feelings, and activities associated with the trauma.
8. Verbalize an understanding of the treatment rationale for PTSD.	1. Educate the client about how effective treatments for PTSD help address the cognitive, emotional, and behavioral consequences of PTSD using cognitive and behavioral therapy approaches. 2. Assign the client to read psychoeducational chapters of books or treatment manuals on PTSD that explain its features, development, and treatment (e.g., *Overcoming Post-traumatic Stress Disorder* by Smyth or *Reclaiming Your Life from a Traumatic Experience: A Prolonged Exposure Treatment Program Workbook* by Rothbaum, Foa, & Hembree.)

(*continued*)

Objectives	Interventions
9. Identify, challenge, and replace biased, negative, and self-defeating thoughts resulting from the trauma.	1. Explore the client's schema and self-talk that mediate his/her trauma-related fears; identify and challenge biases; assist him/her in generating appraisals that correct for the biases and build confidence in them. 2. Assign the client to keep a daily log of automatic thoughts associated with themes of threat and danger (e.g., "Negative Thoughts Trigger Negative Feelings" in the *Adult Psychotherapy Homework Planner*, 2nd ed., by Jongsma); process the journal material to challenge distorted thinking patterns with reality-based thoughts and to generate predictions for behavioral experiments. 3. Reinforce the client's positive cognitions that foster a sense of safety and security and decrease fearful and avoidance behavior (see "Positive Self-Talk" in the *Adult Psychotherapy Homework Planner*, 2nd ed., by Jongsma). 4. Assign the client a homework exercise in which he/she identifies fearful self-talk tests (through behavioral experiments) the predictions from these dysfunctional thoughts, and creates reality-based alternatives; review and reinforce success, providing corrective feedback for failure (e.g., *Overcoming Post-traumatic Stress Disorder* by Smyth).
10. Participate in trauma-focused Prolonged Exposure Therapy.	1. Utilize prolonged exposure to process memories of the trauma at a client-chosen level of detail for an extended period of time (e.g., 60–90 minutes); repeat in future sessions until distress reduces and stabilizes (see *Prolonged Exposure Therapy for PTSD: Emotional Processing of Traumatic Experiences-Therapist Guide* by Foa, Hembree, & Rothbaum; or *Posttraumatic Stress Disorder* by Resick & Calhoun). 2. Assign the client a homework exercise in which he or she does self-directed exposure to the memory of the trauma.
11. Participate in present-focused exposure therapy involving safe, but currently feared activities.	1. Direct and assist the client in constructing a fear and avoidance hierarchy of trauma-related stimuli. 2. Utilize *in vivo* exposure, in which the client gradually exposes him- or herself to objects, situations, or places negatively associated with the trauma. 3. Assign the client a homework exercise in which he/she does an exposure exercise and records responses (see "Gradually Reducing Your Phobic Fear" in the *Adult Psychotherapy Homework Planner*, 2nd ed., by Jongsma, or *Overcoming Post-traumatic Stress Disorder* by Smyth); review and reinforce progress; problem-solve obstacles.

Objectives	Interventions
12. Learn and implement calming and coping strategies to manage challenging situations related to trauma.	1. Teach the client strategies from Stress Inoculation Training (SIT), such as relaxation, breathing control, covert modeling (i.e., imagining the successful use of the strategies), and/or role-playing for managing fears until a sense of mastery is evident (see *Clinical Handbook for Treating PTSD* by Meichenbaum).
13. Learn and implement strategies to prevent relapse of PTSD.	1. Provide a rationale for relapse prevention that discusses the risk and introduces strategies for preventing it. 2. Discuss with the client the distinction between a lapse and relapse, associating a lapse with a temporary setback and relapse with a return to a sustained pattern of thinking, feeling, and behaving that is characteristic of PTSD. 3. Identify and rehearse with the client the management of future situations or circumstances in which lapses could occur. 4. Instruct the client to routinely use strategies learned in therapy (e.g., continued everyday exposure, cognitive restructuring, problem-solving), building them into his/her life as much as possible. 5. Develop a coping card on which coping strategies and other important information can be kept (e.g., steps in problem-solving, positive coping statements, reminders that were helpful to the client during therapy). 6. Schedule periodic maintenance or "booster" sessions to help the client maintain therapeutic gains and problem-solve challenges.

APPENDIX **B**

Chapter Review Test Questions and Answers Explained

Chapter 1: What is Posttraumaic Stress Disorder?

1. Which of the following does not represent one of the three categories of diagnostic *symptoms* of PTSD?

   A. Experiencing an event that involved threatened death
   B. Feeling of detachment or estrangement from others
   C. Irritability or outbursts of anger
   D. Recurrent distressing dreams of the event

      A. *Correct*: Exposure to a traumatic event is not a symptom, but rather what triggers the three categories of PTSD *symptoms*.
      B. *Incorrect*: This represents a symptom from the *avoidance/numbing* category.
      C. *Incorrect*: This represents a symptom from the *hyperarousal* category.
      D. *Incorrect*: This represents a symptom from the *intrusive recollection* category.

2. The DSM diagnosis, "Posttraumatic Stress Disorder, Acute (309.81)," means that the symptoms of PTSD have been present for how long?

   A. Less than one month
   B. More than one month, but less than six months
   C. More than one month, but less than three months
   D. More than six months

      A. *Incorrect*: Symptoms of PTSD must be *at least* one month in duration.
      B. *Incorrect*: The diagnosis means that symptoms are of less than three months' duration.

C. *Correct*: The diagnosis means that symptoms are of less than three months' duration.

D. *Incorrect*: The diagnosis means that symptoms are of less than three months' duration.

Chapter 2: What Are the Six Steps in Building a Treatment Plan?

1. The diagnosis of PTSD requires the evidence of hyperarousal, but clients may experience this in different ways. For example, some will have a sleep disturbance; others may be irritable or startle easily. In which step of treatment planning would you record these features of your particular client?

   A. Creating short-term objectives
   B. Describing the problem's manifestations
   C. Identifying the primary problem
   D. Selecting treatment interventions

   A. *Incorrect*: Hyperarousal is a feature or symptom manifestation, not an objective for the client to achieve.

   B. *Correct*: Features, also referred to as behavioral definitions, expressions, or manifestations, of a problem for the particular client are described in Step 2 of treatment planning: Describing the problem's manifestations.

   C. *Incorrect*: Hyperarousal is a feature or symptom manifestation of the primary problem of PTSD.

   D. *Incorrect*: Hyperarousal is a feature or symptom manifestation, not a therapist's action designed to help the client achieve his or her objective(s).

2. The statement "Identify, challenge, and change biased self-talk supportive of depression" is an example of which of the following steps in a treatment plan?

   A. A primary problem
   B. A short-term objective
   C. A symptom manifestation
   D. A treatment intervention

   A. *Incorrect*: The primary problem (Step 1 in Treatment Planning) is the summary description, usually in diagnostic terms, of the client's primary problem.

   B. *Correct*: This is a short-term objective (Step 5 in Treatment Planning). It describes the desired actions of the client in the treatment plan.

   C. *Incorrect*: Symptom manifestations (Step 2 in Treatment Planning) describe the client's particular expression (i.e., manifestations or symptoms) of a problem.

D. *Incorrect*: A treatment intervention (Step 6 in Treatment Planning) describes the therapist's actions designed to help the client achieve therapeutic objectives.

Chapter 3: What Is the Brief History of the Empirically Supported Treatments Movement?

1. Which statement best describes the process used to identify empirically supported treatments (ESTs)?

   A. Consumers of mental health services nominated therapies.
   B. Experts came to a consensus based on their experiences with the treatments.
   C. Researchers submitted their works.
   D. Task groups reviewed the literature using clearly defined selection criteria for ESTs.

      A. *Incorrect*: Mental health professionals selected ESTs.
      B. *Incorrect*: Expert consensus was not the method used to identify ESTs.
      C. *Incorrect*: Empirical works in the existing literature were reviewed to identify ESTs.
      D. *Correct*: Review groups consisting of mental health professionals selected ESTs based on predetermined criteria such as well-established and probably efficacious.

2. Based on the differences in their criteria, in which of the following ways are well-established treatments different than those classified as probably efficacious?

   A. Only probably efficacious treatments allowed the use of single case design experiments.
   B. Only well-established treatments allowed studies comparing the treatment to a psychological placebo.
   C. Only well-established treatments required demonstration by at least two different, independent investigators or investigating teams.
   D. Only well-established treatments allowed studies comparing the treatment to a pill placebo.

      A. *Incorrect*: Both sets of criteria allowed use of single subject designs. Well-established required a larger series than did probably efficacious (see II under Well-Established and III under Probably Efficacious).
      B. *Incorrect*: Studies using comparison to psychological placebos were acceptable in both sets of criteria (see IA under Well-Established and II under Probably Efficacious).

C. *Correct*: One of the primary differences between treatments classified as well-established and those classified as probably efficacious is that well-established therapies have had their efficacy demonstrated by at least two different, independent investigators (see V under Well-Established).

D. *Incorrect*: Studies using comparison to pill placebos were acceptable in both sets of criteria (see IA under Well-Established and II under Probably Efficacious).

Chapter 4: What Are the Identified Empirically Supported Treatments for Posttraumatic Stress Disorder?

1. Which of the following is not a trauma-focused intervention for PTSD?

   A. Cognitive processing therapy (CPT)
   B. Eye movement desensitization and reprocessing (EMDR)
   C. Prolonged exposure (PE)
   D. Stress inoculation training (SIT)

      A. *Incorrect*: CPT involves exposure and cognitive restructuring of trauma memories.
      B. *Incorrect*: EMDR involves imaginal exposure to selected images of the trauma.
      C. *Incorrect*: Prolonged exposure involves imaginal exposure to memories of the trauma.
      D. *Correct*: SIT involves several interventions intended to facilitate the client's current adaptive functioning.

2. Which form of exposure is used *prominently* in trauma-focused treatments for PTSD?

   A. Imaginal exposure
   B. Live exposure (*in vivo*)
   C. Simulated exposure (role-played)
   D. Virtual reality exposure

      A. *Correct*: Although other forms of exposure may be used in the treatment of PTSD, imaginal exposure is used prominently when working with memories of the trauma.
      B. *Incorrect*: Although live exposure (*in vivo*) is used in the treatment of PTSD, often to present-day stimuli associated with the trauma, imaginal exposure is used prominently when working with memories of the trauma.

C. Although simulated or role-played exposure may be used in the treatment of PTSD, often in preparation for live exposure to present-day stimuli associated with the trauma, imaginal exposure is used prominently when working with memories of the trauma.
D. Although virtual reality exposure has shown promise in initial studies, particularly for creating war-associated simulations, imaginal exposure is used prominently when working with memories of the trauma.

Chapter 5: How Do You Integrate Empirically Supported Treatments into Treatment Planning?

Assessment/Psychoeducation

1. At what point in therapy is psychoeducation typically conducted?

   A. At the end of therapy
   B. During the assessment phase
   C. During the initial treatment session
   D. Throughout therapy

      A. *Incorrect*: Psychoeducation is done throughout therapy.
      B. *Incorrect*: Psychoeducation is done throughout therapy.
      C. *Incorrect*: Psychoeducation is done throughout therapy.
      D. *Correct*: Well, you know the answer.

Prolonged Exposure

1. Which of the following is a primary goal of prolonged exposure?

   A. A change from maladaptive to adaptive appraisals of the trauma experience
   B. Extinction of the emotional response to memories of the trauma
   C. Insight into the origin of the distress
   D. Unihibited expression of the distress associated with the trauma

      A. *Incorrect*: This goal is more consistent with cognitive therapy.
      B. *Correct*: Exposure therapy aims to extinguish conditioned fear.
      C. *Incorrect*: The goal of insight is more consistent with therapies from the psychoanalytic tradition.
      D. *Incorrect*: This objective was characteristic of fad therapies from the 1960s, most notably primal scream therapy.

Cognitive Therapy

1. In cognitive therapy, clients are often asked to test the validity of biased fearful thoughts and beliefs against alternatives that correct for the bias. This is often done by converting the thoughts into predictions and then testing them

through "real-life" exercises to see which prediction is best supported. These exercises are called:

A. Behavioral experiments
B. Conflict-resolution
C. Exposure exercises
D. Problem-solving
 A. *Correct*: Behavioral experiments are typically used to test the validity of biased versus alternative predictions.
 B. *Incorrect*: Conflict resolution refers to a commonly taught set of communication skills for managing conflicts.
 C. *Incorrect*: Exposure refers to a specific technique aimed at fear reduction through repeated exposure to what is feared.
 D. *Incorrect*: Problem-solving refers to a commonly taught skill used to address problems in a systematic manner, as well as a type of therapy that teaches these skills.

Cognitive Processing Therapy

1. Which of the following homework exercises is most consistent with cognitive processing therapy (CPT)?

A. Doing a relaxation exercise
B. Doing an exposure to a currently feared situation
C. Listening to an audiotaped description of the traumatic event
D. Participating in a pleasurable activity
 A. *Incorrect*: CPT is more focused on cognitive restructuring and imaginal exposure, and does not emphasize this intervention.
 B. *Incorrect*: CPT focuses more on past-focused, imaginal exposure than present-focused, live exposure.
 C. *Correct*: This is a common homework assignment in CPT, and a form of imaginal exposure.
 D. *Incorrect*: This intervention is more consistent with behavior therapy for depression.

Live Exposure/Exposure *in vivo*

1. Which of the following therapeutic assignments is most consistent with exposure *in vivo*?

A. Listen to a narrative account of the traumatic experience, and record thoughts and feelings.
B. Write a description of the traumatic experience, include associated thoughts and feelings.

C. Watch a film unrelated to the trauma, that you enjoy.
D. Visit a site that is safe, but similar to one associated with the trauma.
   A. *Incorrect*: This assignment is more consistent with past-focused treatments (e.g., cognitive processing therapy, prolonged exposure).
   B. *Incorrect*: This assignment is more consistent with past-focused treatments (e.g., cognitive processing therapy).
   C. *Incorrect*: Although present-focused, this assignment is more consistent with the scheduling of pleasurable activities seen in behavioral therapy for depression.
   D. *Correct*: Conducting present-focused activities associated with current fear and avoidance is consistent with exposure *in vivo*.

Stress Inoculation Training

1. Which of the following best describes the goal of stress inoculation training (SIT)?

   A. Improving a client's adaptation to the current environment
   B. Improving a client's calming skills
   C. Improving a client's cognitive coping skills
   D. Improving a client's communication skills
      A. *Correct*: SIT is a present-focused therapy, the goal of which is to improve the client's current adaptive functioning.
      B. *Incorrect*: Although this objective may be part of the treatment plan consistent with SIT, it is only one means to the goal of improving the client's current adaptive functioning.
      C. *Incorrect*: Although this objective may be part of the treatment plan consistent with SIT, it is only one means to the goal of improving the client's current adaptive functioning.
      D. *Incorrect*: Although this objective may be part of the treatment plan consistent with SIT, it is only one means to the goal of improving the client's current adaptive functioning.

Eye Movement Desensitization and Reprocessing

1. EMDR is a trauma-focused intervention. Through what primary therapeutic technique does the treatment desensitize clients to memories of the trauma?

   A. Repeated exposure to images associated with the trauma
   B. Repeated pairing of relaxation with images of the trauma
   C. Repeated reading of a description of the trauma experience
   D. Repeated describing by the client of the trauma experience

A. *Correct*: The EMDR procedure asks client to repeatedly imagine scenes associated in memory with the trauma.
B. *Incorrect*: EMDR does not pair relaxation with exposure, a procedure more consistent with systematic desensitization.
C. *Incorrect*: EMDR does not use reading as a form of exposure, a procedure more consistent with cognitive processing therapy.
D. *Incorrect*: Although the client does describe what they are witnessing in their imagination during EMDR, the procedure works with the images and associated thoughts and feelings. The procedure of repeatedly describing the trauma is more consistent with prolonged exposure.

Chapter 6: What Are Considerations for Relapse Prevention?

1. James is nearing the end of his treatment for PTSD. For several weeks he has successfully been completing exposures to situations associated with the trauma. His therapist gives him a homework assignment that asks him to list future situations that might challenge him to revert back to his old fearful and avoidant way of coping. They plan to review the list and develop a plan for managing the challenges effectively. Which consideration in relapse prevention is depicted in this example?

A. Developing a coping card
B. Distinguishing between lapse and relapse
C. Encouraging routine use of skills learned in therapy
D. Identifying high-risk situations for a lapse

A. *Incorrect*: This is a technique used by some clients to help them remember key therapeutic points and strategies outside of therapy.
B. *Incorrect*: This is a psychoeducational intervention designed in part to help prevent misinterpretation of potentially manageable setbacks as an unmanageable relapse.
C. *Incorrect*: This intervention is designed to transport skill use into everyday applications, not just ones that represent a higher risk for relapse.
D. *Correct*: The vignette describes identifying high-risk situations. James and his therapist will then review and develop a plan for managing them.

STUDY PACKAGE
CONTINUING EDUCATION
CREDIT INFORMATION

Evidence-Based Treatment Planning for Posttraumatic Stress Disorder

Our goal is to provide you with current, accurate and practical information from the most experienced and knowledgeable speakers and authors.

Listed below are the continuing education credit(s) currently available for this self-study package. *Please note: Your state licensing board dictates whether self study is an acceptable form of continuing education. Please refer to your state rules and regulations.*

COUNSELORS: PESI is recognized by the National Board for Certified Counselors to offer continuing education for National Certified Counselors. Provider #: 5896. We adhere to NBCC Continuing Education Guidelines. This self-study package qualifies for **1.0** contact hours.

SOCIAL WORKERS: PESI, 1030, is approved as a provider for continuing education by the Association of Social Work Boards, 400 South Ridge Parkway, Suite B, Culpeper, VA 22701. www.aswb.org. Social workers should contact their regulatory board to determine course approval. Course Level: All Levels. Social Workers will receive **1.0** (Clinical) continuing education clock hours for completing this self-study package.

PSYCHOLOGISTS: PESI is approved by the American Psychological Association to sponsor continuing education for psychologists. PESI maintains responsibility for these materials and their content. PESI is offering these self- study materials for **1.0** hours of continuing education credit.

ADDICTION COUNSELORS: PESI is a Provider approved by NAADAC Approved Education Provider Program. Provider #: 366. This self-study package qualifies for **1.0** contact hours.

Procedures:

1. Review the material and read the book.

2. If seeking credit, complete the posttest/evaluation form:

    -Complete posttest/evaluation in entirety; including your email address to receive your certificate much faster versus by mail.

    -Upon completion, mail to the address listed on the form along with the CE fee stated on the test. Tests will not be processed without the CE fee included.

    -Completed posttests must be received 6 months from the date printed on the packing slip.

Your completed posttest/evaluation will be graded. If you receive a passing score (70% and above), you will be emailed/faxed/mailed a certificate of successful completion with earned continuing education credits. (Please write your email address on the posttest/evaluation form for fastest response) If you do not pass the posttest, you will be sent a letter indicating areas of deficiency, and another posttest to complete. The posttest must be resubmitted and receive a passing grade before credit can be awarded. We will allow you to re-take as many times as necessary to receive a certificate.

If you have any questions, please feel free to contact our customer service department at 1.800.844.8260.

PESI LLC
PO BOX 1000
Eau Claire, WI 54702-1000

Evidence-Based Treatment Planning for Posttraumatic Stress Disorder

PO BOX 1000
Eau Claire, WI 54702
800-844-8260

For office use only
Rcvd. ____________
Graded ____________
Cert. sent ____________

Any persons interested in receiving credit may photocopy this form, complete and return with a payment of $15.00 per person CE fee. A certificate of successful completion will be sent to you. To receive your certificate sooner than two weeks, rush processing is available for a fee of $10. Please attach check or include credit card information below.

Mail to: PESI, PO Box 1000, Eau Claire, WI 54702 or fax to PESI (800) 554-9775 (both sides)

CE Fee: $15: (Rush processing fee: $10) **Total to be charged** ____________

Credit Card #: ____________ **Exp Date:** ____________ **V-Code*:** ____________

(*MC/VISA/Discover: last 3-digit # on signature panel on back of card.) (*American Express: 4-digit # above account # on face of card.)

Name (please print): ____________ (LAST) ____________ (FIRST) ____________ (M.I.)

Address: ____________ Daytime Phone: ____________

City: ____________ State: ____________ Zip Code: ____________

Signature: ____________ Email: ____________

Date Completed: ____________ Actual time (# of hours) taken to complete this offering: _____hours

Program Objectives After completing this publication, I have been able to achieve these objectives:

Objective		
1. Explain the process and criteria for diagnosing posttraumatic stress disorder.	1. Yes	No
2. List the six steps in building a clear psychotherapy treatment plan.	2. Yes	No
3. Examine how empirically supported treatments for posttraumatic stress disorder have been identified.	3. Yes	No
4. Identify the objectives and treatment interventions consistent with those of identified empirically supported treatments for posttraumatic stress disorder.	4. Yes	No
5. Describe how to construct a psychotherapy treatment plan and inform it with objectives and treatment interventions identified as empirically supported treatments for posttraumatic stress disorder.	5. Yes	No
6. Identify common considerations in the prevention of relapse of posttraumatic stress disorder.	6. Yes	No

PESI LLC
PO BOX 1000
Eau Claire, WI 54702-1000

ZNT043390

CE Release Date: 2/11/2011

Participant Profile:

1. Job Title: ______________________ Employment setting: ____________________

1. According to psychiatric classification system criteria for the diagnosis of posttraumatic stress disorder, exposure to the traumatic stressor is followed by a response involving symptoms from which of the following symptom categories?
A. Avoidance/numbing, hyperarousal, and intrusive recollections
B. Avoidance/numbing, depression, and hyperarousal
C. Avoidance/numbing, depression, and intrusive recollections
D. Depression, hyperarousal, and intrusive recollections

2. In some cases, the emergence of posttraumatic stress disorder symptoms following exposure to a traumatic event may be delayed.
A. True
B. False

3. A psychotherapy treatment plan contains statements such as, "Experiences frequent nightmares," "describes a reliving of the event through dissociative flashbacks," and "intentionally avoids thoughts, feelings, or discussions related to the traumatic event." These statements constitute which of the following elements of a psychotherapy treatment plan?
A. Behavioral definitions
B. Primary problems
C. Short-term objective
D. Therapeutic interventions

4. As mentioned in the program, several reviewers of the psychotherapy treatment outcome literature for posttraumatic stress disorder have identified trauma-focused interventions as having well-established efficacy. Which of the following is NOT one of the trauma-focused interventions identified by these reviewers?
A. Cognitive Processing Therapy
B. Eye Movement Desensitization and Reprocessing (EMDR)
C. Prolonged exposure therapy
D. Stress inoculation Training

5. Which of the following research supported treatments for posttraumatic stress disorder involves individually tailored cognitive behavioral interventions designed to improve current adaptive functioning?
A. Cognitive Processing Therapy
B. Eye Movement Desensitization and Reprocessing (EMDR)
C. Prolonged exposure therapy
D. Stress inoculation Training

6. A therapist asks her client with posttraumatic stress disorder (PTSD) to write a description of the meaning of the traumatic event (i.e., an impact statement). Once this narrative is written, the client will be asked to read and discuss the impact statement. This task will be revisited as therapy progresses. This type of intervention is most characteristic of which of the following research-supported treatments for PTSD?
A. Cognitive Processing Therapy
B. Eye Movement Desensitization and Reprocessing (EMDR)
C. Prolonged exposure therapy
D. Stress inoculation Training

7. A therapist and his client with posttraumatic stress disorder agree that the client will try to engage in a currently avoided activity associated with a previous trauma experienced by the client. In session, they use a guided self-dialogue procedure in which they discuss preparing for the activity, managing its demands, managing feelings during the activity, and afterward reviewing how the client did. They will repeat this activity toward the goal of overcoming the client's current fear and avoidance. This intervention is most consistent with which of the following research-supported treatments for posttraumatic stress disorder?
A. Cognitive Processing Therapy
B. Eye Movement Desensitization and Reprocessing (EMDR)
C. Prolonged exposure therapy
D. Stress inoculation Training

8. A client with posttraumatic stress disorder (PTSD) is asked to hold in his mind's eye a pre-selected image associated with the trauma and monitor change in thoughts, emotions, and physical sensations associated with it while simultaneously engaging in a distracting task. This intervention is a common component of which of the following research-supported treatments for PTSD?
A. Cognitive Processing Therapy
B. Eye Movement Desensitization and Reprocessing (EMDR)
C. Prolonged exposure therapy
D. Stress inoculation Training

9. According to this program, an intervention commonly used in relapse prevention is to identify and rehearse coping with high-risk times for relapse.
A. True
B. False

10. Which of the following best describes the approach to creating an evidence-based treatment plan for posttraumatic stress disorder that is recommended in this program?
A. The therapist conducts relaxation training
B. The therapist conducts exposure to currently avoided situations
C. The therapist incorporates into therapy the objectives and interventions consistent with research-supported treatments for posttraumatic stress disorder
D. The therapist incorporates into therapy the use of an objective measure of disruptive behavior to track treatment progress